Scheming

I0807201

Scheming

A Social History of Glasgow Council Housing, 1919–1956

Seán Damer

EDINBURGH
University Press

Edinburgh University Press is one of the leading university presses in the UK. We publish academic books and journals in our selected subject areas across the humanities and social sciences, combining cutting-edge scholarship with high editorial and production values to produce academic works of lasting importance. For more information visit our website: edinburghuniversitypress.com

© Seán Damer, 2018, 2020

Edinburgh University Press Ltd
The Tun – Holyrood Road
12 (2f) Jackson's Entry
Edinburgh EH8 8PJ

First published in hardback by Edinburgh University Press 2018

Typeset in 11/15 Adobe Garamond by
Servis Filmsetting Ltd, Stockport, Cheshire

A CIP record for this book is available from the British Library

ISBN 978 1 4744 4056 1 (hardback)
ISBN 978 1 4744 4057 8 (paperback)
ISBN 978 1 4744 4058 5 (webready PDF)
ISBN 978 1 4744 4059 2 (epub)

The right of Seán Damer to be identified as author of this work has been asserted in accordance with the Copyright, Designs and Patents Act 1988 and the Copyright and Related Rights Regulations 2003 (SI No. 2498).

For Tony – gentleman and scholar

And what's there? Hardly anything but houses. Just architectural dumps where they unloaded the people like slurry. Penal architecture. Glasgow folk have to be nice people. Otherwise, they would have burned the place to the ground years ago.

William McIlvanney (1979), *Laidlaw*, p. 32

Contents

Tables and Figures

TABLES

FIGURES

Acknowledgements

The Economic & Social Research Council-funded project (R000231241) upon which this book is based began some time ago, from 1988 to 1991, in the (then) Centre for Housing Research of the University of Glasgow, where I was Senior Research Fellow. Some of this research has already been published. A general critical discussion of the development of Glasgow council housing was contained in my book on the Moorepark housing scheme, known as the 'Wine Alley',[1] and also in my *Glasgow: Going for a Song*.[2] Much original material on Blackhill was published in a University of Glasgow Discussion Paper,[3] and on Hamiltonhill in an *Urban Studies* journal article.[4] However, over time, colleagues have put persistent pressure on me to publish the results of this research in its entirety. My colleagues, Professors David McCrone and Richard Rodger of the University of Edinburgh, urged me continuously to publish my rich empirical material. I am particularly grateful to David for his long-term editorial, financial, moral and sociological support for this project. I would also like to acknowledge the continuous support offered to me in the course of the original research by Professor Duncan McLennan, then Director of the Centre for Housing Research, who as an economist demonstrated that he did not lack sociological imagination.

The tenancy structure for Mosspark was analysed by Ann McGuckin, Research Assistant on this project, 1989–90, who was also involved in the research on Mosspark and Blackhill. The tenancy structures of all the other schemes were analysed by Linda Hartshorne, Research Assistant 1990–2. I am most grateful to Linda for her reliable and painstaking work.

I would also like to acknowledge the sterling work done by Deirdre Campbell in retyping all the material in my ESRC Report, as the original disks had become corrupted.

Colleagues and friends who commented on all or part of this book include Anni Donaldson, Tony Fallick, Alistair Fraser, Dave McCrone, Willy Maley, Alan Middleton, Gerry Mooney, John Nolan and Valerie Wright, and I am most grateful to them, while absolving them of any responsibility for errors of fact or interpretation. Thanks also to Mike Shand for the map of the schemes.

I would like to thank the staff of the City Archives, Parliamentary Papers section, and Special Collections in the Mitchell Library, Glasgow – and not for the first time – for their cheerful, expert and invaluable assistance in the course of the original research, and in the preparation of this book.

I would also like to acknowledge the literally dozens of Glasgow council tenants who spoke to me willingly if not uncritically of their experience, and also the numerous Corporation officials who recounted their experiences in allocating and managing the city's council houses.

The photographs of the woman in the slum interior (The Virtual Mitchell C67); Mosspark Boulevard (C2237); Hamiltonhill housing (C2274.tif); the Hamiltonhill Social Centre (C2277.tif); West Drumoyne shops and

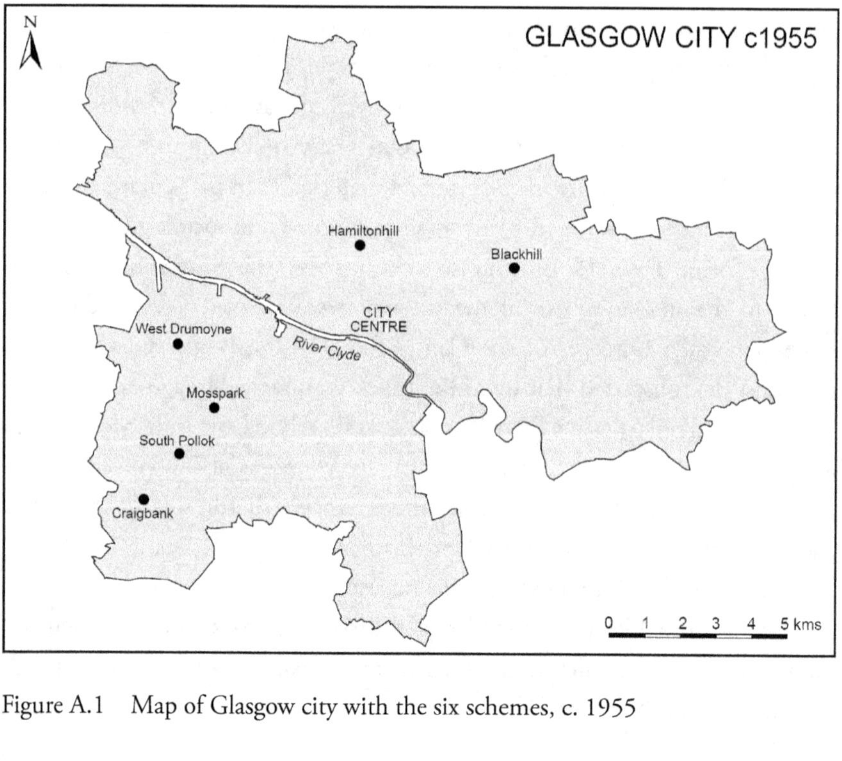

Figure A.1 Map of Glasgow city with the six schemes, c. 1955

housing (Glasgow Housing Department Review of Operations 1919–1937); Fairhill Avenue, South Pollok (D-AP9/6/10); Diagram 1 – Mosspark layout (D-AP9/11/31); Diagram 2 – Hamiltonhill layout (D-AP9/11/20); and Diagram 3 – Blackhill layout (D-AP9/11/18), are reproduced by permission of Glasgow Life (Glasgow Museums and Collections): Glasgow City Archives. The cover photograph of the kids in Blackhill was taken by John Nolan and is reproduced with his permission. The photograph of Prestwick Street, Craigbank, was taken by Gavin McGinlay and found on the Internet; in spite of considerable effort, I have been unable to trace him.

Notes

1. Damer, S. (1989), *From Moorepark to 'Wine Alley': The Rise and Fall of a Glasgow Housing Scheme*, Edinburgh University Press.
2. Damer, S. (1990), *Glasgow: Going for a Song*, Lawrence & Wishart.
3. Damer, S. (1992), *'Last Exit to Blackhill:' The Stigmatisation of a Glasgow Housing Scheme*, University of Glasgow Centre for Housing Research Discussion Paper No. 37.
4. Damer, S. (2000), '"Engineers of the Human Machine": The Social Practice of Council House Management in Glasgow, 1895–1939', *Urban Studies*, Vol. 37, No. 11, 2007–26.

Preface

For all that Glasgow's radical council housing programme was internationally famous in both the interwar and post-Second World War years, its treatment by academics is underwhelming. While the basic economic, social administrative and constructional aspects of local housing policy in this period have been dealt with adequately,[1] detailed housing history seems to have almost disappeared from the general area covered by the rubric of 'Urban Studies'. Insofar as it has been retained, it has been left to architectural historians, which some might see as a fate worse than death given their propensity to talk only in design terms, use impenetrable jargon, and their apparent ignorance of the fact that a house is meant to constitute a home for human beings as opposed to Le Corbusier's bombastic 'machine for living in'.[2]

The controversial and politically important story of the development of Glasgow's council housing, particularly in the interwar years, has simply not been told systematically. In other words, that story has been depoliticised. But this will not do. The story of council housing in Glasgow is the story of class-struggle, and the intensity of that struggle, and its potential for disruption at the level of both the local and national state, can be gauged from the following apocalyptic quotation from a 1923 book. Although it is not unknown to serious students of Glasgow's interwar housing, it is worth repeating:

> The Red Clyde, the smouldering danger of revolution in Glasgow, owing to the swift development of political affairs in Britain, has ceased to be a local anxiety, and become an interest and an alarm to the whole civilised world . . . There is something deeply wrong with the Clyde; the whole middle-class of England knows it, though hardly in detail; the motive is

> adequate, real, dangerous, that sends in repeated menace, to every successive Parliament, the same bitter group of extreme Left Members, irrespective of the changing political mood of the rest of the country, to kill with their fierce interruptions any restful optimism of the remainder of the House. The Red Clyde will remain the focus of English politics, until it has been cured, or definitely appeased; or until first Scotland, then industrial England becomes fully infected by it, with momentous effects on Britain, the British Empire, and the rest of the world. The mainspring of the trouble, the root grievance of the Clyde, is Housing . . .[3]

Further, nostalgic and kitsch memoirs aside,[4] there is really nothing which tells the story of the lived experience of thousands upon thousands of Glaswegian working-class tenants in their new council housing schemes in an accessible language. Given that the allocation of a new council house was one of the most important life events for many of these tenants, this lacuna is astonishing. This book intends to fill the gap, not least because five of the six schemes discussed in this book have already been demolished, and their story nearly lost.

Then, in recent years, there has been a pernicious effort to label council housing schemes as ghettos, housing only the allegedly socially inadequate 'parasites-upon-the-welfare-state' so beloved of Tory rhetoric. A striking example of this tendency is the 2010 BBC Scotland television series *Scheme*, purporting to portray the lives of typical tenants of the Onthank and Knockinlaw housing schemes in Kilmarnock. This rebarbative and voyeuristic series reeks of *nostalgie de la boue*, and has been subjected to a telling critique by Law and Mooney.[5] Another indicator of the demonisation of council housing schemes is the evolution of the word 'schemie' in Scotland to signify a tenant from such estates. A straw poll of friends in my local suggests that this term originated in the 1970s. There can be no doubt that it is a pejorative label, as a cursory glance at the Internet will demonstrate. Another glance at the Internet will reveal an astonishing number of blogs and websites in which former tenants of these Glasgow schemes reminisce warmly and in detail about life within them, and seek information about their history. There can be no doubting the importance of these schemes to the people who lived in them.

Scheming intends to both fill the lacuna, and correct the offensive labelling, by providing a detailed analysis of six different Glasgow council housing schemes, set in the context of both national and local housing policy. It will argue that the balance of class forces at both levels shaped the financing, location, design, tenanting and management of these schemes. It will also argue that the cultural survival of Victorian Octavia Hill-type maternalistic housing management ideology into the postwar years in Glasgow had the unintended consequence of reproducing and amplifying social segregation within the city. Thus this book is, in perspective, sociological; in content, historical, with proper attention paid to qualitative and quantitative materials in the shape of census data, official records and oral histories.

Why start in 1919? The Housing & Town Planning Act of that year was responsible for introducing what became known subsequently as 'council housing', and the end date of 1956 is selected because thereafter Glasgow turned mainly to multi-storey tower-block building in an effort to solve its housing problems. The literal and metaphorical visibility of these 'multis', and the controversy surrounding their fitness for purpose, moved the whole debate about council housing onto another level, so that it became easy to confuse working-class housing and multis. My point is that there is a much older and finer-grained debate which came to define the council housing question in Glasgow. Fortunately, my colleague Dr Valerie Wright of the University of Glasgow is compiling an oral history of high-rise living in the city, along with other researchers.[6] What follows is a brief discussion of how my original research was carried out.

After I graduated in Sociology in 1968 from the University of Edinburgh – the very first class of Sociology graduates in the history of Scotland – my first job was as a Planning Officer in the Corporation of Glasgow's Planning Department. At that time, Glasgow was undergoing massive social and structural change. Twenty-nine 'Comprehensive Development Areas' (CDAs) had been declared, within which nearly 100,000 dwellings were to be demolished, with some 60 per cent of their inhabitants to be housed elsewhere. They moved to the four huge peripheral schemes of Castlemilk, Drumchapel, Easterhouse and Pollok, and to the New Towns of Cumbernauld and East Kilbride, with some even winding up in Glenrothes, in Fife.[7] A result of this strategy was that the Inner City wards were hugely depopulated.

Not everyone in Glasgow agreed with this policy of wholesale demolition. On the one hand, there was a group of young graduates in the Social Sciences – mainly Geography and Sociology – within the Planning Department which felt that the social consequences of this policy had not been thought through. And on the other, tenants of some neighbourhoods which were to be comprehensively redeveloped, particularly in Govan and Partick – districts with strong community characteristics – made it clear that they wanted to stay where they were. And on top of all this, within the Corporation, there was inter-departmental friction as some older Departments were suspicious of the Town Planners with their newfangled ideas. So in an effort to make sense of this, my colleagues and I liaised with our opposite numbers in other Departments, particularly Housing Management, as it was then known. This liaison greatly facilitated my subsequent research into the 'Wine Alley' and other housing schemes. So in 1988, when I started the research which lies behind this book, I already knew, and was known by, a good number of key officials, particularly in the Housing Management Department. Therefore it was a relatively simple matter to trace officials who had been involved in the early management of the six schemes I elected to study.

As far as original tenants of the six schemes were concerned, the officials nominated some, some were contacted by personal relationships, and 'word of mouth' found others. The sample within each scheme was not random, and was constituted by a 'snowballing' effect. What I did try to do was interview as many pioneer tenants in each scheme as possible; the interviews were conducted between 1989 and 1991. The bulk of the interviews was conducted by me, a few by Anne McGuckin and Linda Hartshorne. In the transcripts of interviews in the text, interviews by Ann are designated 'AM', by Linda 'LH' and by myself 'SD'. All these interviews, both with pioneer tenants of the six schemes and contemporary housing officials, were conducted using a standardised interview schedule, tape-recorded and transcribed. The C90 audio-cassettes on which they were recorded were then lodged in the Glasgow City Archives, and have been digitised subsequently. In this book, the names of interviewees, and names used within the interview transcripts, are all pseudonyms unless specifically stated otherwise.

Notes

1. Brennan, T. (1959), *Reshaping a City*, Glasgow: Grant; Butt, J. (1978), 'Working-Class Housing in Glasgow, 1900–1939', in I. McDougall (ed.), *Essays in Scottish Labour History*, Edinburgh: John Donald; Checkland, S. (1981), *The Upas Tree*, University of Glasgow Press; Cramond, R. (1964), *Allocation of Council Houses*, University of Glasgow Social & Economic Studies Occasional Paper No. 1, Edinburgh: Oliver & Boyd; Gibb, A. (1982), *The Development of Public Sector Housing in Glasgow*, University of Glasgow Centre for Urban & Regional Research Discussion Paper No. 6, Glasgow; Gibb, A. (1983), *Glasgow: The Making of a City*, Croom Helm; Maclennan, D. and A. Gibb (1988), *Glasgow: No Mean City to Miles Better*, University of Glasgow Centre for Housing Research Discussion Paper No. 18, Glasgow; Morgan, N. (1989), '"£8 Cottages for Glasgow citizens": Innovations in municipal house-building in Glasgow in the inter-war years', in R. Rodger (ed.), *Scottish Housing in the Twentieth Century*, Leicester University Press.
2. Horsey, M. (1990), *Tenements and Towers: Glasgow Working-Class Housing 1980–1990*, HMSO; McKean, C. (1993), 'Between the Wars', in P. Reed (ed.), *Glasgow: The Forming of the City*, Edinburgh University Press.
3. Bolitho, W. (1924), *Cancer of Empire*, Putnam's, p. 13.
4. For example, Hanley, C. (1984), *Dancing in the Streets*, Corgi; Paterson, B. (2008), *Tales from the Back Green*, Hodder & Stoughton; Weir, M. (1973), *Shoes Were for Sunday*, Macmillan.
5. Law, A. and G. Mooney: (2011/12), '"Poverty Porn" and *The Scheme*: Questioning Documentary Realism', *Media Education Journal*, 50, Winter, pp. 9–12.
6. Abrams, L., A. Kearns, V. Wright and B. Hazely, *Housing, Everyday Life and Well-Being Over the Long-Term: Glasgow c. 1950–1975*; ongoing research project.
7. Maver, I., 'Neighbourhoods', in www.theglasgowstory.com. Accessed 23 November 2017.

1

Introduction

1919: The National Housing Situation

The 1919 Housing & Town Planning Act, the 'Addison' Act, placed a statutory duty on local authorities to survey the general working-class housing needs of their areas and submit development plans.[1] Following the 1919 Tudor Walters Report, the Act laid down generous criteria for the design of this housing: they were generally to be four-in-a-block cottage-type dwellings, the smallest of which were to be of three apartments. The subsidy was equally generous: all losses not met from the revenue of a penny rate – 4/5th of a penny in Scotland – would be covered by the Treasury, provided the schemes had been approved by the Ministry of Health or, in Scotland, the Scottish Board of Health. However, these houses were to be let at an economic rent. The Act constituted legislation designed to respond to wartime labour agitation on housing issues, especially rents, and also end-of-the-war industrial unrest, particularly on Clydeside, mutinies among un-demobilised soldiers in the Army, a police strike and the threat of a General Strike. In Swenarton's telling phrase, it was an 'insurance against revolution'.[2] The state was not only responding to internal social unrest but also was mindful of the revolutionary activity in Russia, as the contemporary debates in the House of Commons make plain. It is hardly surprising that Lloyd George wanted half-a-million houses built in three years, a phenomenal target.

But although this housing was supposed to meet the 'general needs' of the working class, its generous design criteria made it expensive to build, resulting in high rents which were beyond the capacity of all but the most skilled workers. A consequence of the rushed nature of this Act was that it was ill-drafted and the subsidies ruinously expensive. It is hardly surprising that the 1923 'Chamberlain' Act of the Tory government effectively tried to return the provision of working-class housing to the market, and, specifically, to ensure that council housing existed only in a 'residual' role. A central assumption was that the housing problem was a temporary one, and thus its subsidy ran only to October 1925. It was designed essentially to stimulate private enterprise construction, and so its subsidy for council housing, quite cynically slashed to £6 per house, was released only if it could be proved that private enterprise could not meet the demand for working-class housing. Given that the provision under the 1919 Act scarcely dented the surface of the demand, it can readily be seen that the Chamberlain Act was blatant ideology, an attempt to return to the Victorian principle of a free housing market. Thus, in Glasgow only 2,052 houses in the 'Ordinary' category were constructed under this Act. However, it did contain a clause aimed specifically at the slums – Glasgow seized the initiative and 6,546 houses in Rehousing schemes were constructed.

But when the balance of class forces swung in favour of Labour with the election of the Ramsay MacDonald government of 1924, this gave Clydeside socialist John Wheatley, his Minister of Housing, the chance to force through the 1924 Housing Act. The key point of this Act was that it restored the power of local authorities to build working-class housing without having to demonstrate that it could not be provided by private enterprise. The subsidy was to be £9 per house for forty years, rents were pegged at the pre-war level, private enterprise was encouraged to build working-class houses, and Wheatley did a deal with the trade unions which facilitated the rapid expansion of the construction industry. The principle of council housing as a social service had been established; the state was now committed to subsidising the rents of the workers in such housing. Imaginative as Wheatley's Act was, and successful as it was in responding to the 'general needs' of the working class, the problem of poverty-stricken slum-dwellers had not even been touched. The rents in Wheatley Act houses were simply beyond their reach. The problem which not even he had resolved was a differential rents policy, that is, an economic strategy for constructing adequate council houses at rents which the different sections of the working class could afford. The old question of not being seen to subsidise the rents of the poor out of the rents of the more affluent remained unanswered.

This problem was addressed by the 1930 'Greenwood' Act, which was specifically aimed at slum-clearance. It did this by subsidising the number of people cleared from slums and rehoused. But John Wheatley was now dead, the working-class movement had been defeated in the General Strike, Tory interests prevailed in Ramsay MacDonald's National Government, and the cost of both labour and building materials had risen exponentially. Thus the design and finishing of the tenemental council houses built under the 1930 Act were markedly inferior to those built under earlier legislation, and the density per acre much higher than in estates built under the 1919 Act. Furthermore, their monotonous layout was a potent visual symbol of the low esteem in which contemporary slum-dwellers were perceived. That perception was a conflation of slums and their inhabitants whereby 'those people' – the slum-dwellers – were signified as the problem rather than their rotten housing. However, even though this legislation was aimed specifically at slum-dwellers, it proved largely ineffective in tackling the dense tracts of grossly overcrowded slums in cities like Glasgow. So, in 1935, a Housing Act was passed which was aimed specifically at 'decrowding', by introducing strict criteria defining overcrowding. However, the subsidy for the new houses for these 'clearees' was less generous than in the 1930 Act, and would prove to have profound consequences in the long term.

1919: The Glasgow Situation

In 1919, working on the basis of the 1890 Housing of the Working Classes Act, Glasgow Corporation estimated that it needed 57,000 new council houses immediately. This figure was broken down as follows:

(i) 21,000 – relief of overcrowding;
(ii) 3,000 – replacement of houses which should be closed and demolished;
(iii) 7,000 – to rehouse those displaced by Improvement Schemes under the 1890 Housing Act;
(iv) 15,000 – to meet estimated natural population increase between 1919 and 1922;
(v) 5,000 – to meet the needs of new industries;
(vi) 5,500 – to meet the needs of demobilised servicemen;
(vii) 500 – temporary houses.[3]

This housing strategy explicitly included provision for rehousing slum-dwellers, as can be seen from (iii) above. But the 1890 Act was enabling legislation only. It empowered local authorities to declare Improvement Areas for slum-clearance and rebuilding, with no subsidy for the latter activity, which could only be carried out with the express approval of the Local Government Board in Scotland. Hence, no large-scale action anywhere in the country, including Glasgow, was initiated under this legislation. The typical operations were in penny packets. Nonetheless, by 1919 Glasgow had declared at least two Improvement Areas, one in the Cowcaddens and the other in Garngad.

After the 1919 Housing & Town Planning Act was passed, the Corporation of Glasgow was quick off the mark. There were two reasons for this. First, a series of enquiries into Glasgow's housing had made it ineluctably clear that the situation was critical. The Minutes of Evidence of the 1885 Royal Commission on the Housing of the Working Classes; the 1892 Glasgow Presbytery Commission on the Housing of the Poor; the 1904 Glasgow Municipal Commission on the Housing of the Poor; and the 1917 Royal Commission on the Housing of the Industrial Population of Scotland, Rural and Urban, had painted a grim picture of gross overcrowding in very small one-roomed ('single-end') and two-roomed ('room-and-kitchen') houses with outside toilets in the common stair, in densely packed tenemental neighbourhoods with inadequate sanitation, sunlight and ventilation. The public health consequences of such private housing were catastrophic, as was remarked in detail by Glasgow's Medical Officers of Health, Sanitary Inspectors and Inspectors of the Poor, who gave expert evidence to these Commissions. As early as 1888, Dr James Burn Russell, Glasgow's distinguished Medical Officer of Health, had drawn attention to these health consequences in a talk entitled 'Life in One Room'. His language was almost poetic:

> Of all the children who die in Glasgow before they complete their fifth year, 32 per cent. die in houses of one apartment; and not 2 per cent. in houses of five apartments and upwards. There they die and their little bodies are laid out on a table or on the dresser, so as to be somewhat out of the way of their brothers and sisters, who play and sleep and eat in their ghastly company.

> From beginning to rapid-ending the lives of these children are short parts in a continuous tragedy.[4]

This situation was caused by the practice of keeping the corpse in the house for three days before burial. It was usually kept on the family bed by day and on the table by night.

Second, the working-class movement in the city, spearheaded by the Independent Labour Party (ILP), had been agitating since well before the First World War on the housing issue. Noting that private enterprise had failed signally to solve the problem of affordable working-class housing, it demanded state subsidies, and radical improvements in its design. ILP Councillor John Wheatley's 1913 pamphlet '£8 Cottages for Glasgow Citizens' demonstrated what could be done with a modest subsidy, attracted national attention and galvanised debate. The ILP and its sister organisation, the Scottish Labour Housing Association, not to mention the grassroots organisation of women in bodies such as the South Govan Housing Association, had been central to the furore over the opportunistic wartime hiking of rents. In 1915 this resulted in a militant city-wide rent strike, which forced the government to introduce the 1915 Rents & Mortgage Interest Restrictions Act, a significant victory for the working-class movement.[5] And 1919 had started with the 'Bloody Friday' riot in George Square on 31 January.

There could be no doubt that the Corporation of Glasgow was well aware of the political volatility of the housing question. In 1919 it established a Housing Department whose first Director was Peter Fyfe, Chief Sanitary Inspector of the city; his pamphlet on the 'Housing of the Labouring Classes' was a benchmark contribution to the debate.[6] This new Department, which also contained a Chief Engineer and a Chief Architect, was responsible for building housing, and promoted a Housing Exhibition which included an architectural competition for working-class housing; £6,000 was donated anonymously for prize money by 'a Citizen'.[7] It was also involved in considerable experimentation with construction materials. The City Improvements Department, a continuation from the City Improvement Trust of the pre-war years, was responsible for letting and managing the new housing. In other words, the provision of council housing was *the* major item in Glasgow's inter-war municipal policy. This was admitted explicitly by the Corporation itself:

> The housing of the population in this City is the paramount problem which faces the Town Council. They have many problems awaiting solution, but none of them is of equal urgency and importance to this one, and all their efforts are required to find a speedy and satisfactory means of supplying homes for our people.[8]

This admission is hardly surprising as the 1911 Census showed that 62.1 per cent of a population of just over one million lived in grossly overcrowded houses of two rooms or less.[9] In short, Glasgow had more and worse slums than any other city in Britain. But it is to be noted that while the Corporation of Glasgow was aware of the problem, it was inexperienced in both a large-scale construction programme, and the management, of council housing. As Morgan has pointed out, it was almost incredible that the Corporation should propose such a massive municipal building programme without the appropriate administrative infrastructure.[10] In the decades before the First World War, it was Glasgow's architects and builders who made money out of housing.

The post-First World War Corporation of Glasgow was controlled by the Moderate Party, an uneasy Tory–Liberal coalition whose *raison d'être* was to keep Labour out of office, which it did successfully until 1933. But it set about the construction of council houses with a will, and between 1919 and 1939, 54,289 were built. However, within the Corporation there was constant warfare between the Moderates, the party of the Glasgow middle class, and the ILP, the party of the working class, as to the design, size, location, rent, tenanting and management of this housing. The intensity of this can be gauged by the fact that following a heated debate about rent levels in the new council housing, the Minutes noted:

> . . . the Chairman, in respect of the disorder arising, quitted the chair, and the meeting accordingly stood adjourned.[11]

Three days later, when the meeting was continued, the Minutes recorded:

> At this stage, Councillor Shinwell [ILP], being guilty of obstructive behaviour and having disregarded the authority of the Chairman . . . [he] suspended the said Councillor Shinwell for the remainder of the sitting of the house.[12]

By 1939 the outcome of this warfare was the establishment of a rigid three-tier league table of council housing schemes in Glasgow, each more or less socially homogenous. At the top of the table was the 'Ordinary' category, containing houses usually built under the provisions of the 1919 Housing & Town Planning Act and the 1923 Housing Act. Next was the 'Intermediate' category, containing houses built mainly under the provisions of the 1924 Housing Act. And at the bottom was the 'Slum-Clearance/rehousing' category, built under the provisions of the 1930 and 1935 Housing Acts. While these housing schemes were financed by the different subsidies provided by the different Housing Acts, they also looked different, were different in size, contained markedly different groups of tenants, and were both perceived and managed as different moral communities, characterised by whether or not their tenants were perceived as 'deserving'. Any council tenant in Glasgow could tell at a glance into which category a housing scheme fell, and to which category he or she could aspire. In this book, Mosspark is an exemplar of the 'Ordinary' type of scheme, West Drumoyne of the 'Intermediate' and Blackhill of the 'Slum-Clearance'.

The basic development of these schemes has already been described adequately by the economists, economic historians, geographers and historians from the University of Glasgow, and the architects and architectural historians, quoted earlier. But these studies are descriptive and empiricist to a degree. They neither touch upon the bitter local class struggles about these schemes, nor their management and social trajectories, nor the lives of their tenants. Only one of these studies mentions the tripartite tier in their classification, and then only in terms of the rent structure.[13] And they certainly do not reflect the sheer drama of the story of council housing development in Glasgow. Recent books about Glasgow do not even mention council housing.[14] This lack of a systematic history and sociology of the city's council housing schemes means the story was very nearly lost forever. This book intends to ensure that that story is preserved. In selecting six schemes for analysis, it will provide detailed case studies from each of the three categories in the league table, plus a unique experimental scheme. A synthesis of archival and oral history data, from both pioneer tenants and contemporary housing officials, will provide the systematic analysis absent from the literature to date. It will also demonstrate that Glasgow's development of its three-tier system, and attendant housing management ideology and practice, was unique in Britain, that the lever of such policy was social class, and that it had unintended consequences which reverberate to this day. The analysis of the six different housing schemes is presented chronologically.

Notes

1. Housing, Town Planning, &c. Act 1919 (c35.). As the social administrative details of this and subsequent housing legislation have already been discussed in an extensive literature, what follows in this chapter is a summary of the key points. Critical references include: Bowley, M. (1945), *Housing and the State, 1919–1944*, Allen & Unwin; Burnett, J. (1986), *A Social History of Housing, 1815–1985*, Methuen; Daunton, M. (1990), *Housing the Workers, 1850–1914: A Comparative Perspective*, Leicester University Press; Malpass, P. (2015), *Housing and the Welfare State: The Development of Housing Policy in Britain*, Palgrave Macmillan; Merrett, S. (1979), *State Housing in Britain*, Routledge & Kegan Paul; Swenarton, M. (1981), *Homes Fit for Heroes: The Politics and Architecture of Early State Housing in Britain*, Heinemann Educational.
2. Swenarton (1981), op. cit., p. 111.
3. Glasgow Corporation *Minutes*, Special Committee on Housing & General Town Improvement, Print No. 26, 15 October 1919, pp. 2317ff: Draft Housing Scheme.
4. Chalmers, A. K. (1905), *Public Health Administration in Glasgow: A Memorial Volume of the Writings of James Burn Russell, B.A., M.D., Ll.B.*, Glasgow: James MacLehose & Sons, p. 196.
5. See Damer, S. (1980), 'State, Class and Housing: Glasgow 1885–1919', in J. Melling (ed.), *Housing, Social Policy and the State*, Croom Helm, for a detailed discussion of this process.
6. Fyfe, P. (1899), *Housing of the Labouring Classes*, A Lecture Delivered Before the Glasgow & West of Scotland Architectural Craftsmen's Society, Printed by Order of the Corporation of the City of Glasgow, by Robert Anderson.
7. Glasgow Corporation *Minutes*, Print No. 27, 12 October 1921, p. 2723.
8. *Glasgow: Its Municipal Undertakings and Enterprises, 1923*, Corporation of Glasgow, p. 63.
9. *Glasgow Census*, 1911.
10. Morgan, N. (1989), '"£8 cottages for Glasgow citizens": Innovations in municipal house-building in Glasgow in the inter-war years', in R. Rodger (ed.), *Scottish Housing in the Twentieth Century*, Leicester University Press, p. 130.

11. Glasgow Corporation *Minutes*, Special Committee on Housing and General Town Improvement, Print No. 11, 18 March 1920, p. 1067.
12. Ibid., Print No. 11, 25 March 1920, p. 1070.
13. Butt (1978), op. cit.
14. Crawford, R. (2013), *On Glasgow and Edinburgh*, The Belknap Press of Harvard University Press; Taylor, A. (ed.) (2016), *Glasgow: The Autobiography*, Birlinn.

2

Mosspark: Homes Fit for Heroes?

Post-First World War Housing in Glasgow

In the city of Glasgow in 1919, with a population of just over one million, the housing situation was atrocious, as the immensely sad Figure 2.1 demonstrates. Roughly two-thirds of Glaswegians lived in houses of not more than two rooms. About one-fifth lived in single-ends and almost half-a-million in rooms-and-kitchens, the vast majority with outside toilets. In pockets of the worst slums, in the 'backlands', the population density was a staggering 400 persons to the acre. In Britain as a whole, as well as in Glasgow, private enterprise had proved itself unwilling or incapable of solving the working-class

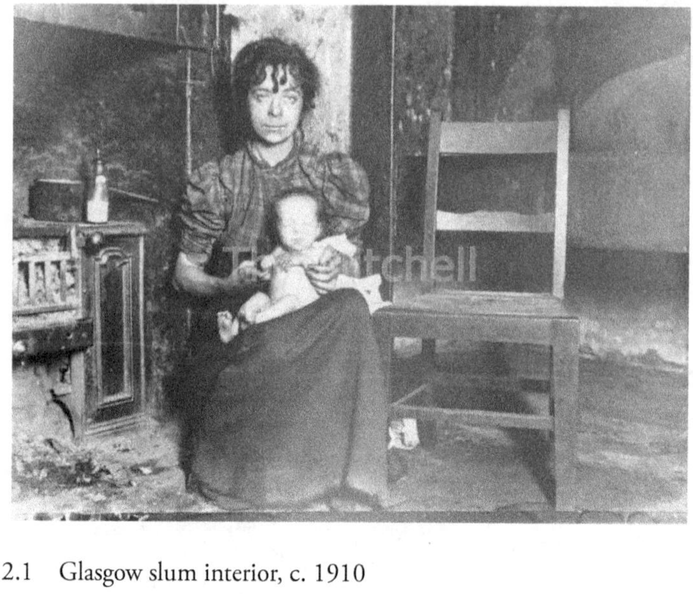

Figure 2.1 Glasgow slum interior, c. 1910

housing problem; there simply wasn't enough profit in it. This was the context for Lloyd George's famous promise of 'homes fit for heroes', and the passing of the 1919 Housing & Town Planning Act. This Act *required* local authorities, for the first time, to survey the housing needs of their areas and specify plans for adequate housing provision. All losses in excess of a 4/5d rate in Scotland were to be borne by the Treasury for a period of two years, provided the plans had been approved by the Scottish Board of Health. Although subsequently criticised as being poorly drafted, the 1919 Act was a watershed in the provision of municipal housing for the working class; there could be no retreat from this provision.

Mosspark: Site Development

The Mosspark area was chosen as the site of one of Glasgow's pioneering housing schemes under the 1919 Act. It was not the first scheme; that honour fell to Riddrie. But Mosspark was *the* prestigious scheme, and retains a substantial element of that prestige to this day. The Corporation had in fact purchased the 'Lands of Mosspark', comprising some 175 acres, in 1909. This was to be laid out as a municipal 18-hole golf-course, but the First World War intervened. The first housing plan for the Mosspark site was submitted to the Local Government Board and approved in April 1919. The next step in its development was its adoption in a general Town Planning Scheme for the south-west of the city passed by the Corporation of Glasgow on 20 October 1919, under Section 1 of the 1919 Act. The Mosspark scheme was originally for 1,502 houses in 174 acres, or just under nine houses to the acre. The site was triangular, with fine vistas to Bellahouston Park to the north, and the Old Pollok Estate to the south, the ancestral home of the Maxwell family. It rose from 50 feet above sea level to a hill of 155 feet in the centre.

The Corporation Minutes show that the building schedules for Mosspark were ready for tendering by June 1920, were approved by the Scottish Board of Health in October of that year, and Sir John MacTaggart of MacTaggart & Mickel was awarded the contract. Even before construction commenced, the Town Clerk was receiving letters from prospective tenants asking to be put on the waiting list.[1] At £1,800,000 for 1,510 houses (£65 million in contemporary value), Mosspark was a very big housing scheme for its time. Building began in February 1921 and was completed by June 1924, the works being supervised by Mr Fyfe, the new Director of Housing. It was a huge project, involving a labour force of 1,300 men at its height, and necessitating the construction of a new railway depot and a narrow-gauge slip-line into the site from the Glasgow and South Western Railway line to the south of the scheme.

The hilly nature of the scheme presented some engineering problems with regard to sewage disposal. These were solved by the construction of a pumping station. The houses were constructed of brick and roughcast, but MacTaggart was given permission to include 252 experimental houses built of concrete blocks. Of the 1,510 houses eventually built, there are 593 of three apartments (39 per cent); 644 of four apartments (43 per cent); and 273 of five apartments (18 per cent). Thirteen different types of house design were used in the scheme, and the general layout followed the principles of the 'garden suburb', Raymond Unwin's Town Planning notion which was in vogue at the time. Such residential suburbs were to contain housing at low density, wide tree-lined roads, gardens and woods, with hedges rather than walls separating houses, and were to be quiet.[2]

Each house contained a bathroom with bath, sink and WC; a scullery with a gas cooker, gas boiler and washing tub; a coal cellar; a larder; press (cupboard) accommodation; and a minimum of two bedrooms. Electric light was supplied, and hot water was available from a boiler behind the living-room fire. The houses cost £1,150 each to build, on average. Rents varied from £28 per annum for a three-apartment house to £44 per annum for a five-apartment house. These high rents automatically excluded most manual working-class tenants from Mosspark, for in the early 1920s the maximum wage for a skilled manual worker was about £2 per week, and for a labourer £1.2.0d. The net density was nine houses to the acre. The first houses were opened by Lord Provost Thomas Paxton on 15 September 1921. At this juncture, the seven and a half miles of new roads were unlaid, nor was there any street lighting. Nevertheless, all the houses were let by October 1923.

Tenanting Mosspark

By 1921 there were almost 14,000 names on the council house waiting list in Glasgow. Obviously the Corporation had to have a procedure to select its tenants for the new Mosspark scheme. A formal house allocation system existed, based on a points system.

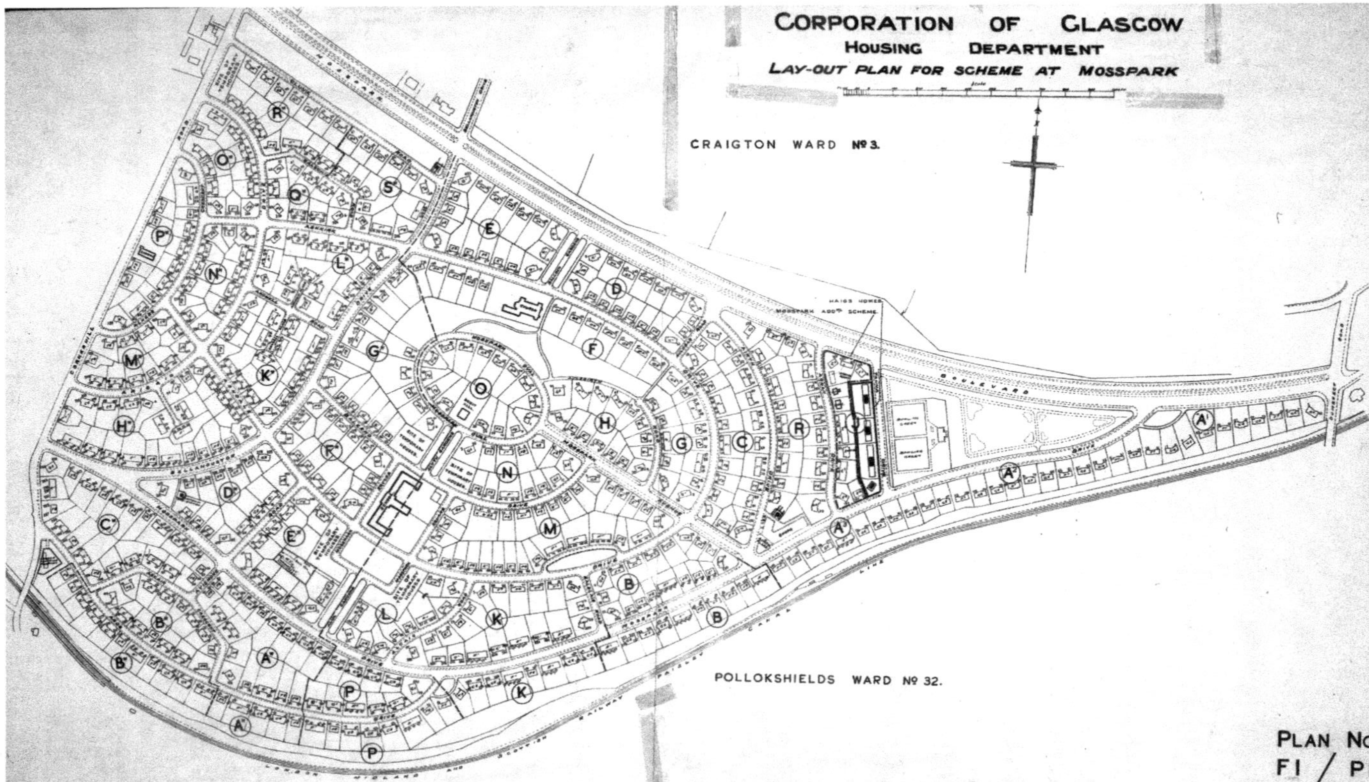

Figure 2.2 Mosspark layout

The City Improvements Department – responsible for house letting and management – allocated a unit value to each of the following items:

- Early application
- Nearness of work or residence to new house
- Wages or salary under £6 per week
- Married
- With one child
- With two children
- Demobbed Men
- Over two years' service
- Resident in Glasgow over 18 years
- In lodgings or in a single room
- In an overcrowded house

Thus the maximum was eleven points: one point for each item above. Few candidates, however, had more than eight or nine points, and the majority had fewer. Prospective tenants were selected from those with a minimum of six points. 'Undesirable tenants' were not to be accepted, and this was to be ascertained by a home visit assessing such nebulous criteria as cleanliness, respectability and decency – entirely subjective criteria. In other words, it was extremely difficult to qualify for one of these houses, and it was meant to be.

A large number of representations were made to the Corporation by Councillors asking for priority in housing allocation to be given to ex-servicemen, particularly the disabled. Such priority was ratified by the Corporation at its meeting of 30 January 1919. It was reiterated by the Scottish Board of Health in its 1921 Annual Report, which also stressed the ability of future tenants to pay their rents, as well as requiring their 'respectability'. By 1921 the Town Clerk, Sir John Lindsay, was being deluged by letters either asking to be put on the waiting list, or recommending someone for a council house.[3] The former were frequently from ex-servicemen, recommended by Glasgow's property elite – lawyers, property-owners and house-factors.

By 1922, these applications, now on the City Improvements Department's printed application form, had become a torrent.[4] Examples are:

> A managing foreman, married with two children over 10, earning £9.0.0d. per week, currently living in two rooms. His referee is Sir John Lindsay, Glasgow's Town Clark, and a business-card is attached from a Dundee Baillie saying that this applicant is his son.
>
> A law clerk, married with one child over 10, an ex-serviceman earning £300.0s.0d. p.a., and living in two rooms and a kitchen. His referee is also Sir John Lindsay.
>
> An electrical engineer in the Corporation Electricity Department, married with three children over 10, with a family income of £450.0.0d. p.a., and living in a four-apartment house. His referee is the Chief Engineer of the Electricity Department.
>
> The Secretary to the General Manager of the Corporation Gas Department, married with two children under 10, earning £230.0.0d p.a. plus a bonus of £105.0.0d. p.a., living in a three-apartment house. His referee is a firm of Glasgow lawyers.
>
> A JP's Clerk in the Corporation, married with one child above 10, earning £4.5.0d. per week, a Special Constable during the war, 'living with friends'. His referee is Sir Thomas Wilson in Glasgow Corporation.
>
> An Engineer, married with one child under 10, an ex-serviceman, no income declared. His referee is the Head of the City Improvements Department.
>
> A Water-Surveyor in the Corporation, married with two children over 10, earning £292.0.0d p.a., living in a five-apartment house. No referee is given.

Indeed, by 1924 the Town Clerk himself is recommending prospective tenants to the Clerk of the City Improvements Department Committee responsible for house allocation. Here is an example:

> Housing – Mr William Paterson. The above named is anxious to get one of the Corporation's houses in view of his approaching marriage. I understand you have already intervened on his behalf, but treat this as a special case – one of our own staff, and see Mr Ewan or Mr Nicholson and report to me.[5]

To put it simply, as far as Mosspark was concerned, the issue was not what you knew, but who you knew.

This evidence, and the occupational structure of the original Mosspark tenants (see the table at the end of this chapter), strongly suggest that the formal allocation system was overshadowed by an informal system based on the following considerations:

- a well-developed 'commonsense' understanding of the concepts of 'desirable' and 'undesirable' tenants;
- steady, rather than high, income;
- its corollary, the moral superiority of white-collar over blue-collar workers;
- the prioritisation of Corporation white-collar and professional employees, and other public service workers.

This unsophisticated elaboration of the formal points system resulted in numerous opportunities for value judgements by, or pressure upon, critical gatekeepers such as the City Improvements Department Clerk responsible for the selection of tenants.

The result of this informal allocation system was a tenancy structure in Mosspark which had nothing to do with the 'general needs of the working class' as specified in the 1919 Act. The Sub-Let Book (i.e. rental roll) for Mosspark demonstrates that the first tenants were overwhelmingly white-collar workers and professionals, including clerks, businessmen, commercial travellers, doctors, dentists, solicitors, house-factors, engineers, bank cashiers and tellers, schoolteachers, Inspectors of the Poor, merchant marine officers, Customs and Excise officers, and a 'rubber planter'.[6] Clerks and schoolteachers constituted the two biggest occupational groups by far. An interloper was a certain 'trade-union organiser' named Emanuel Shinwell, a prominent Red Clydesider and militant ILP Councillor. There was no Resident Factor in Mosspark or any other 'Ordinary' scheme in Glasgow, and rents were paid quarterly at the central office at 20 Trongate. Such an arrangement would have been impossible for even skilled manual workers.

The few manual workers who eventually did get a house in Mosspark before the Second World War had to fight for it, as the following interview makes clear:

SD: How did your father get that house in Mosspark?

Mrs G: Dad came out of the [First World] War with an artificial leg, and they had four children and then they had Annie after. And that was like five girls and my father and mother in a room-and-kitchen. And there was no possibility of getting a house. My mother was a fighter, and my mother went up to the Housing Department *every* day, *every single* day. And finally they got so disgusted with her that they gave her a house, but she didnae take just any house. She took the house that *she* wanted. She said, 'My husband lost a leg fighting for this War and we have five children and we want a decent house in a decent place to live. That was what he went and fought for.'

The original occupational structure of Mosspark is summed up in the following comments selected from numerous tape-recorded interviews in the scheme:

> This place was full of professionals – teachers, government officers, and Corporation workers. Everybody knew that you had to be earning £5 per week to get a house.

And:

> There were lawyers, bankers, school teachers, and people worked in the Corporation.

And:

> Mosspark has always maintained until recently a high level of intelligence. We were, if I may put it snobbishly, a white-collar community.

And:

SD: What were your neighbours like?

Mrs G: Well on one side of us the man worked in Coates [the thread-mill in Paisley]. They were fairly well off. On the other side of our house there was a young couple who had the house for about three months before they came into it. They had a little boy after a while and Jenny [the speaker's sister] tells the story of waking up one morning to find a horse in the back garden – a horse for the wee boy.

SD: A horse for riding, rather than a working horse?

Mrs G: It wasn't a working horse. It was for riding. They were really snooty, you know. What was it she called him, some awfully fancy name? Then we discovered his name was Isaac! [The wee boy, not the horse!]

My mother used to get awfully angry. She [the neighbour] had me in occasionally baby-sitting, and the house was marvellous. The beds were beautiful, and everything was beautiful. We weren't very well off, we weren't quite – well, we were furnished but we didn't have the niceties that she had. My mother used to say: 'That's making you restless . . .'

Across the road were the Grahams and the father in that house was the Manager of the [Corporation] Transport Department. There were very few of them like us. And down in Auldbar Road there was a family and he was an official in the Corporation. They were nearly all Corporation officials that came first – and schoolteachers. Very few manual workers.

These comments confirm the belief expressed by several interviewees that a suspiciously high number of original Mosspark tenants *were* Corporation officials. It also tells us that this respondent's mother did not want her daughter to become too aspirational, to get 'ideas above her station' as a result of proximity to this better-off neighbour.

In any event, reactions to this skewed allocation policy came at both local and national level, orchestrated by the ILP. Numerous Glasgow newspapers commented upon Mosspark's élite status.[7] Embarrassing questions were asked in both the Corporation of Glasgow and the House of Commons. As early as 1922, Councillor Rosslyn Mitchell (ILP) put the following question to the Convenor of the Special Committee on Housing and General Town Improvement:

> Will the Convenor state how many of the houses erected by the Housing Department since 1918 are occupied by ex-soldiers, and how many by persons who are not ex-soldiers?[8]

Two years later, another Councillor asked:

> Is it the case that a house in Corkerhill Road, Mosspark, has been let to a member of the Medical Profession, who is the proprietor and occupier of a

house of a rental at £75, at Ladybank Avenue, Craigton, and (b) who was the proprietor up till Whitsuntide of this year, of another house, at a rental of £75, at Dalgarvel Avenue, Dumbreck?[9]

In the same year, *Hansard* records the following exchange, with ILP MPs Harris and Buchanan asking awkward questions:

Mr. J. Harris asked the Minister of Health whether he is aware that many of the subsidised houses in the Mosspark district of Glasgow provided by the Corporation of that city are let to tenants who are in receipt of substantial incomes; and whether he will recommend to the Corporation of Glasgow the advisability in future of making inquiries as to the means of those applying for houses, in order that preference may be given to poorer applicants?
The Secretary for Scotland (Mr. Adamson): I have been asked to reply. I have no information on the financial position of tenants at Mosspark, but I understand that the Corporation of Glasgow have recently had under consideration the question of the letting of houses in their housing scheme, and have adopted certain rules for the regulation of such letting in future which provide *inter alia* for a maximum family income of £350. The houses in question are provided for the working-class generally, and I should hesitate to interfere with the discretion of the local authority in the matter.
Mr. Buchanan: May I ask if it is a fact that they are provided for the working-classes, seeing that the lowest rent chargeable, including rates, amounts to almost £1 a week? Does that not prove that they are denied to the working-classes and that only people with substantial incomes can occupy these houses?
Mr. J. Harris: Is it true that some of the occupants of these houses are in fact registered owners of private motor-cars?
Mr. Buchanan: The right honourable Gentleman said that these houses are for working-class people, but I want to ask, if the rents and rates charged approximate £1 per week, how can working-class people pay the rent, and are they not reserved for well-to-do people?
Mr. Adamson: I have no information as to whether any of the tenants at Mosspark have motor-cars.

Mr. Buchanan: They have.

Mr. Adamson: I have no such information, although the honourable Member may have. With regard to the other point, it is very difficult for certain sections of the working-classes to meet a rent of £1 a week.[10]

Early Community Life in Mosspark

There were three major voluntary associations in Mosspark in the interwar years. These were the Mosspark Parish Church, the Mosspark Tenants' Association and the Mosspark Bowling Club. These will be discussed in turn.

The Mosspark Parish Church was, naturally, Presbyterian, that is, Church of Scotland. But what was important was that this Church prefigured the Union of the Church of Scotland and the United Free Church of 1929. Thus its congregation of 800 contained many members – 60 per cent – of the UF Church. The church building started in a wooden hut in Arran Drive. As a result of vigorous fundraising – and the relative affluence of parishioners – and after obtaining a site from the Corporation, the foundation stone of the new church was laid on 27 June 1925. The *Glasgow Herald* described the ceremony:

> The Masons marched in procession from the temporary church in Arran Drive to the site of the new building at Balloch Gardens, and there the full ritual of applying the tools of the craft, laying the stone, and placing the casket containing memorial documents and coins in the cavity, and the symbolic use of cornucopia and the pouring of wine and oil on the stone was performed.[11]

The *Herald* noted that the Earl of Stair, as Immediate Past Grand Master of Scotland, and Commissioner of the General Assembly of the Church of Scotland, presided, while six Kirk Ministers were involved in the Masonic rites before a large crowd of spectators. It also poured with rain!

These Masonic rituals were a public signal of the religious as well as class characteristics of the new estate. Its territory was clearly not for the unskilled manual worker, which in contemporary Glasgow was synonymous with Irish Catholic. Many observations about this sectarian exclusion were offered openly to me. This speaker is a retired Moderate Party Councillor, a well-known local Tory:

> AB: Well, there was a religious bias – it didn't exist only in Mosspark despite its proximity to Ibrox Park [home ground of Rangers FC] but I think that's dying out in Mosspark – there's not the same religious bias in Mosspark because there's not the same religious-minded people in Mosspark as there used to be.
>
> SD: When you say 'religious bias in Mosspark', what do you mean?
>
> AB: I mean what you know perfectly well I mean – there was bias against Roman Catholics.

And:

> Mrs H: I would say that they [the original tenants] were nearly all Protestants, of the Protestant faith – there weren't any Roman Catholics.

So, in Mosspark, Glasgow's notorious sectarianism was deployed immediately and unapologetically in the allocation of houses.[12] The Church supported a vigorous social life organised around the Junior and Senior Choirs, the Literary and Dramatic Society, the Women's Guild, the Men's Club, the Bible Class, the Guides and Scouts, the Horticultural Society and the Masonic Lodges.

The Mosspark Bowling Club was opened by Baillie Welsh on 30 May 1925, with a membership fee of one guinea. There were over 100 applications for membership. The majority of the original members were also members of the Church, while members of the Kirk Session often duplicated as office-bearers and committee members (known as 'Directors'). The Club went from strength to strength, with a Ladies' Section – meaning the wives of existing members only – being opened in 1930. The (extant) Minutes of the Bowling Club (held in the clubhouse) evince a solidly middle-class language:

> The President extended a cordial welcome to all members and expressed the hope that our dealings would be harmonious as well as pleasant and profitable.

And:

> A vote of thanks to the Committee men terminated the Proceedings of a sederunt which concluded at 11pm.

However, a hiccup in the harmonious proceedings of the Bowling Club occurred when the few ILP members resident in Mosspark complained formally to the Corporation that it might become an exclusive, private club. This objection resulted in a flurry of correspondence between the Town Clerk and the Bowling Club, and the reception of several delegations. The formidable ILP Councillor Paddy Dollan (later to become Lord Provost in 1938) made his objections clear:

> Bailie Dollan . . . was entirely opposed to public funds being used in this particular manner. There was the danger of setting up little exclusive communities, and there was a suspicion throughout the city that they were 'mollycoddling' the people of Mosspark and giving them treatment and conditions which they would not give the people living in slum areas. If they were going to construct bowling greens and tennis courts they should be retained by the Corporation and open to every citizen and not become the exclusive monopoly of the members of particular clubs.[13]

The Town Clerk made it clear that Mosspark Bowling Club was to be open to all tenants in the scheme. In spite of this, one old club member commented in an interview:

> Mr R: The members of the Bowling Club before the War were elderly men, all good businessmen, all good types for the Club, surveyors, bankers. There was only one Catholic in the Club until well after the War. That's what spoiled Mosspark.

Clearly, this member is making the risible proposition that the presence of Catholics was responsible for the decline and fall of Mosspark.

The Mosspark Tenants' Association was founded in November 1925, President, Captain Wilfred Hamilton, and women were well represented on the Committee. It was an active, well-attended organisation which had a membership of over 1,000. The meticulously kept Minute Books for the interwar years show that it agitated about transfers within the scheme, smoke, noise, and obscene language from the adjacent railway yard, the 'oscillation' [swaying] of tramcars, the lack of pillar-boxes and shops, the speeding of cars, the lack of first-class carriages on the local trains, and badly kept gardens, inter alia.[14] It bombarded the Corporation and other public institutions with letters complaining about a variety of services.

> GARAGE ENTRANCES: A petition was read signed by Mr Dunlop, and other garage-owners, in which they drew attention to the Fascist [sic] nature of a letter which they had received from the Director of Housing requesting them to provide slipways at the entrance to their garages. They pointed out that for years they had been expending their energy and cash in improving Corporation property, and that their thanks takes the shape of a curt order to expend more money on more improvements.[15]

The Tenants' Association distanced itself from the ILP-dominated city-wide Federation of (Council) Tenants' Associations, claiming that '. . . we were non-Party and non-sectarian'. The subtext is of course that the Association were Moderates. The Minutes of the Association are emblematic of the middle-class, parliamentary and pompous manner in which the Mosspark tenants conducted their public business as a pressure-group.

In sum, these three voluntary associations mutually reinforced the moral superiority, cultural and religious separation, and social and physical distance which the Mosspark residents perceived themselves as having from other council tenants in Glasgow. These attributes were confirmed and endorsed by subsequent Corporation house-allocation policy in the scheme. This élite status expressed itself politically in a solid Tory vote at both Council and Parliamentary level within Mosspark, a situation which remained unchanged until well after the Second World War. The local Conservative Hall was outside Mosspark physically, but there was no need for special organisation within the scheme, as the Tory vote was simply taken for granted.

Labour – ILP – supporters were not welcome in Mosspark:

> Mrs G: . . . and they started the Socialist Party. Of course they had no premises. And what we used to do was run whist drives in the various

Figure 2.3 Mosspark Boulevard in the 1920s

houses. And then they used to run dances in the Railwaymen's Institute over in Corkerhill. And they got enough then, and they built a hall which is *now* Conservative Rooms – and that was the ILP Hall.

SD: When did the ILP start up?

Mrs G: It must have been shortly after we came here, because their hall was built within five years. I would be about eighteen or nineteen then.

SD: What kind of people were these schoolteachers and Corporation clerks politically?

Mrs G: Oh they were all Tories, again we were in the minority, and again we were the outcasts because we were Socialists.

SD: This became known?

Mrs G: Oh it became known. My father got one or two anonymous letters about 'Communist scum get out of here'.

SD: And that was from people within Mosspark?

Mrs G: It must have been from people within Mosspark.

The above observations might suggest that Mosspark was socially homogenous. While the collective self-perception was definitely one of social superiority, there was in fact complex social differentiation based upon occupational status, and residential sub-area, *within* the scheme. Thus locals state that the cottages of the east end of Mosspark Drive were for professional people and members of the Corporation. Similarly, the houses at the top of the hill, in Mosspark Oval, with their splendid vistas to the north and west, physically as well as socially dominate the scheme. Some streets, such as Ashkirk Drive, contain a high proportion of three-apartment houses at the lowest rental in the scheme, and seem to have been less favoured. Three elderly locals, all original tenants, described the early tenancy patterns thus:

> MN: Along Mosspark Drive, it was nearly all professional people there – at the end of Mosspark Drive.
>
> SD: What sort of street numbers would that be?
>
> LP: The low numbers – where the Councillors were. All the people in the Corporation got a choice. At the beginning of Mosspark, it was all Baillies [magistrates]. There was the Manager of the [Corporation] Gas Department and the Electrical Department.
>
> MN: People from the Corporation got these houses first.
>
> LP: They were all fives [apartments].
>
> EF: It was a nice outlook – over the Bowling Club.

The Church, the Bowling Club and the Tenants' Association were largely patriarchal organisations, and while strategic in conveying the public image of Mosspark as the apogee of the Protestant Ethic, its *internal* specificities were socially policed by the women of the scheme. It was they who had to keep up with the MacJoneses, and they who conveyed the everyday external signs of internal respectability in their neighbouring, shopping and community activities. So the social structure of Mosspark was gendered, just as it had been in the traditional tenements; the women policed each other by gossip. Local women may have attained their dream house, with its own 'front and back door', in a dream scheme, but they had to struggle to maintain their status.

Uniformed maids were not unknown in Mosspark in its early days, and while I found evidence for live-in maids, daily home-helps were much more commonplace. Some of these were working-class girls from Govan.

> SD: In those early years before you went to the nursing, did you know any families that had maids?

Mrs G: Oh yes. I didn't know them personally but I knew of them. There was one up in Balerno Drive and they had a maid. Oh, there were several maids. And they were dressed with their wee black frocks. In the mornings they had their grey dresses on but in the afternoon they had their black dresses on, and their wee frilly aprons and caps.
AM: Do you know where they came from?
Mrs G: Oh they came from Govan.

A 1931 Public Assistance application from a 72-year-old widower in Dennistoun noted that his 24-year-old daughter worked as a 'domestic' in Mosspark, and earned 10s. per week plus one meal per day.[16]

Voluntary associations aside, Mosspark lacked community facilities, and it was not an inconsiderable walk to the nearest pubs, clubs and shops, so the major focus of community life for women focused on intensive socialising in each other's homes – the whole expressed in an almost pioneering spirit:

Mrs G: It was like pioneering. I've heard my mother say – and my father before he died – we were sort of pioneers here . . . I think at the beginning that Mosspark was just virgin soil.

Skills in the tea ritual, and in dress, were vital aspects of women's acceptance in Mosspark, and thereby their families' social standing. Women who could not participate in this intense and competitive socialising – or who were excluded from it – could be employed to enhance participants' status by small-batch baking or cooking for them. It was virtually unheard of for married women in Mosspark to work, and husbands – when they could – as well as children came home at lunchtime. Socialising also involved card-playing, including bridge, in the evenings, which might or might not include a 'wee refreshment', a Scots euphemism for an alcoholic drink. However, this gendered behaviour should not necessarily be seen as constituting female solidarity or empathy; it is just as likely to have been highly competitive.

So in the first couple of decades in the life of the scheme, the picture is one of substantial occupational and residential stability, as Table 2.1 demonstrates. The few families who could not afford the rent in Mosspark appear to have voted with their feet and left the scheme quickly. There seems to have been some modest turnover in the mid-1930s, in terms of both the occupational structure of tenants, and the rate of turnover of tenancies. But for incomers, especially those with young children, the established social life of the scheme could be impenetrable. This family arrived in the early 1930s:

SD: How did your neighbours treat you when you first arrived?
Mrs MacD: It was a long while before they spoke to us . . . They used to look down on you. I think it was because we had a younger family. They didn't want anyone with young children . . . They were just a wee clique up there, very, very, snooty . . .
SD: Did any of the people across the way, or up or down, have small children like yours?
Mrs MacD: No, they were older. Five boys next door, but they were all at College [university]. The boys' mother wouldn't allow them to speak to [my] girls over the fence. Frightened they had any alliances with them.
SD: Is that right?
Mrs MacD: That's true, but when the war came, they unbent a little but not much, but it made a difference to us.

It is apparent that Mrs MacD wanted to be accepted, as it is hard to be an outsider in a place like Mosspark. Discussing the Church, the same housewife said:

Mrs MacD: . . .Very much a select crowd. The same as it is today. They keep their eyes on new people.
Mr MacD: If you're not one of them, they look down their noses at you.

The attitude to children is endorsed by another tenant:

Mrs O: They didn't approve of people with a lot of children. They didn't let houses to them. Children in Mosspark, even now, there's not many children in Mosspark considering the number of people.

A local man, a Moderate Party Councillor in the postwar years and a known Tory, summed up pre-war Mosspark thus:

Mr C: Well, I would describe it as good, law-abiding, church-going society, that went about its work, minding its own business, fraternising with its

> neighbours, and falling out with very few. In other words, an admirable place in which to reside.

Its final atmosphere was described thus:

> Mrs S: They were all very friendly, unlike nowadays, where everybody is on first-name terms. It was always Mrs Mackenzie, Mrs Campbell, Mrs Ferguson, etcetera. There was no familiarity as there is now.

Summary

To sum up: by the end of the 1930s, Mosspark was a hard-working, well-ordered and well-regulated Protestant community, conservative, respectable and sober, predominantly professional and white-collar with a sprinkling of highly skilled manual workers, and with more than a hint of the 'unco guid' [excessive self-righteousness] which can be the hallmark of the Scots Presbyterian. Looking at the occupational table, and amalgamating professional, skilled white-collar and white-collar workers, it can be seen that they constitute 75 per cent of the population in 1926, 73 per cent in 1929 and 62 per cent in 1937. Skilled manual workers rose slightly from 18 per cent of the population in 1926 to 21 per cent in 1937, while unskilled manual workers rose from 0 per cent in 1926 to 6 per cent in 1937. Mosspark was all about the discreet charm of the petty bourgeoisie. It was literally and sociologically a moral community, more than capable of policing both its boundaries and its inhabitants. While there were ex-servicemen in this scheme, there were no unskilled manual workers at all among its first tenants.

In the interwar years, Ward 32, Pollokshields, in which Mosspark was located, returned a continuous stream of Moderate Party Councillors to the Corporation. A Labour Party candidate stood only once, in 1930, and he was trounced.[17] In other words, in terms of municipal politics, this Ward was solidly right-wing.

Table 2.1 Mosspark occupational structure, 1926–1937

% by column	1926	1929	1937
Professionals	16	12	11
Skilled white-collar	28	29	23
Other white-collar	31	32	28
Skilled manual	18	18	23
Unskilled manual	0	2	6
Women*	7	7	10

*This refers to female heads of households for whom no formal occupation is given.

Notes

NB: All references preceded by 'GCA' refer to the Glasgow City Archives.

1. GCA D-TC 8/18: 1919–20.
2. Raymond Unwin's book, *Town Planning in Practice: An Introduction to the Art of Designing Cities and Suburbs* (1909), was hugely influential at the time.
3. GCA D-TC 8/18: 1921–2.
4. Ibid.
5. Ibid., 1923–4.
6. GCA D-CF/3/1. See also GCA D-CF 1.3.
7. See the numerous facetious remarks about Mosspark tenants made in 1923 and 1924 in the weekly magazine *The Baillie*, the house-journal of the Glasgow bourgeoisie, held in the Special Collections Department of the Mitchell Library.
8. GCA: Corporation of Glasgow *Question Book No. 3*, 5 January 1922, quoted in Damer (1990), op. cit., p. 163.
9. Ibid., p. 164.
10. 279 H.C. Deb. 5 s, p. 359, para. 68.
11. *Glasgow Herald*, 25 June 1927.
12. An accessible introduction to this issue is in Gallagher, T. (1987), *Glasgow: The Uneasy Peace: Religious Tension in Modern Scotland*, Manchester University Press.
13. *Glasgow Herald*, 13 June 1924.
14. Mosspark Tenants' Association *Minutes*: GCA TD6 17/1 and 2.
15. Ibid.
16. GCA D-HEW 18/1: Vol. 436:1, Division 1, District 1, Ward No. 1, Divisional Reg. No. 65307.
17. Data derived from the Glasgow Citizens Union annual *Yearbooks*, 1924–39, held in the Special Collections Department of the Mitchell Library: GC324.41443 CIT.

3

Hamiltonhill: A Pioneering Slum-Clearance Scheme

The Legislation

In its 1919 housing strategy, the Corporation of Glasgow had included limited plans for slum-clearance of its own volition. It was enabled to execute these plans under a little-known provision of the 1921 Housing Act. The main purpose of this Act was to abolish the generous subsidies of the 1919 Act, but it also provided an annual grant of £200,000 for the specific purpose of slum-clearances throughout the UK, a provision which seems to have been overlooked totally by both Bowley and Merrett in their studies of British housing legislation.[1]

The portion allocated to Scotland was £30,000.[2] Glasgow's share of this subsidy was £10,000, and it proceeded to construct four small 'Rehousing'/'Slum-Clearance' (the terms were and are interchangeable in Glasgow) schemes at Hamiltonhill, Logan Street, Newbank and Yorkhill.[3] The hierarchy in Glasgow's council housing can be grasped readily when it is realised that the Corporation was able to build four 'Rehousing' schemes for £10,000 while it spent £1.8 million on Mosspark.

In an interesting footnote to history, Glasgow Corporation (and, later, District Council) has consistently got the classification of Hamiltonhill wrong. In all three of its Housing Department's 'Reviews of Operations', and in its index of Glasgow District Council Schemes, Hamiltonhill is recorded as having been built under the provisions of the 1923 Housing Act – as indeed are the other three schemes. This is a curious error given that in its second 'Review of Operations' (1919–37), the date of the tender for Hamiltonhill is given as 3 July 1922.[4]

Site Development

The Hamiltonhill site was quite literally tucked away from view, above the junction of the Forth & Clyde Canal with the branch that continued to the whisky bond at Port Dundas. It was developed very quickly. The Corporation Minutes show that the site – 13 acres at 3/3d per square yard – was acquired in April 1922; the layout of 348 houses was approved in May; and the tenders accepted by the end of July. There were 300 two-apartment and 48 three-apartment houses.[5] The scheme was formally opened in June 1923. The bulk of its first tenants came from slum-clearance areas in the Cowcaddens, notably Muse Lane. This neighbourhood contained 650 people at the staggering density of 1,500 people per acre.[6] The contemporary Scottish Board of Health's Statutory Inquiry into the Corporation's 'Slum-Clearance'/'Rehousing' scheme gives a graphic picture of the housing conditions in Muse Lane. A property in 45 Muse Lane is described thus:

> It is a four-storey tenement, consisting of 28 single-apartment and 3 two-apartment houses. The houses are farmed out, at rentals of 10/- per week for single apartments and 12/- for two apartments. The houses are generally defective in lighting and ventilation. In the ground floor it is only possible to see the sky within eighteen inches of the windows. The walls of the ground floor are damp and the ceilings of the top floor show staining from previous damp. The houses are entered from dark and unventilated lobbies. The floor of the stair landings one up, two up, and three up is worn and open at the joints at certain places.[7]

The Report also notes that the gas had to be kept on all day to provide light in the stair. The local Death Rate was 22.1 as opposed to 15.51 for the city; the respiratory disease rate was 5.7 per 1,000 as opposed to 2.87 for the city; the phthisis (TB) rate was 2.3 as opposed to 1.13 for the city; the Infant Mortality rate was 147.8 as opposed to 112.7; and rickets was common.[8] The Medical Officer of Health, Dr A. K. Chalmers, said:

> Muse Lane has become really the typically bad bit of Glasgow, and has been for a long time.[9]

A *Glasgow Herald* report of 1924 describes the kind of house available in the four new 'Rehousing' schemes. The report actually concerns the opening of the Logan Street scheme, but the houses there were identical to those in Hamiltonhill, except that because of the very small site they were constructed at a much higher density:

> The scheme has been the cause of considerable controversy with the Board of Health in respect of the density being 48 houses to the acre. Each house has a bathroom fitted with a bath, wash-hand basin and wc, and a kitchenette fitted with a fireclay washtub and sink, a coalbunker and a fitment containing a small press. In the living-room there are a dresser and a ventilated food cupboard. An iron bedstead is supplied in one apartment in each house, and blinds are supplied on all windows. This scheme is practically an 'all-gas' scheme as, with the exception of the coal-fire in the interior back-to-back grate in the living room, the other apartments are heated by gas-fires and the lighting in this case is by gas. The main walls of this scheme are double, the outer walls being of natural-faced concrete blocks, and the inner walls of brickwork in cement. The masonry and brickwork of the scheme, as well as the slater work and plaster work has been carried out by the Housing Department Direct Labour. The cost of the houses varied from £228 to £370, and the rents are 28/- for two-apartment houses and 32/- for three-apartment houses, both inclusive of rates.[10]

In Logan Street, the density was 47.8 houses per acre, and in Hamiltonhill – a much bigger site – 27.1. The latter was built by private contractors, the former had a large Direct Labour component. This achieved a saving of between £16 and £19 per house.[11] Those tenants who came to Hamiltonhill from the farmed-out houses of Muse Lane not only gained more space – and a bathroom – they also paid less rent for it.

It is a revealing comment on the desperate nature of the contemporary Glasgow housing market that no sooner had the tenants left the Cowcaddens slums for Hamiltonhill than they were re-occupied by other tenants. Those which were 'farmed-out' houses, now owned by the Corporation, were rapidly re-let. 'Farmed-out' housing existed in poor-quality tenements which had been converted into single-room 'houses', provided with minimal furniture, and let out by the day or week. They constituted a major component of Glasgow slums. One can only suspect collusion between the house-farmer and Corporation Public Health officials. On the one hand the Corporation is supposed to be clearing the slums, while on the other it is permitting the exploitation of poor people by house-farmers. The issue was well enough known to generate a question in the Corporation to the Convenor of the Special Committee on Housing:

> Councillor William McLellan: Have you any knowledge that the slum dwellings from which tenants are being removed to Hamiltonhill are already being re-let to other tenants, and what power has the Corporation to prevent this?[12]

It is worth noting that the small size of the Hamiltonhill houses was a source of heated political controversy within the Corporation. The issue was that while the Corporation wanted to get as many houses as possible onto the small and disadvantaged 'Slum-Clearance' scheme sites, the ILP wanted to adhere to the stated principle of the 1917 Royal Commission that no more small houses should be constructed for workers. The Commission had in fact recommended that nothing smaller than three-apartment houses should be built. The ILP in the Corporation, led by Councillors Wheatley and Stewart, tried to have this enforced in Hamiltonhill, but were defeated both in the Housing Committee and the full Corporation on the vote.[13]

The actual physical *location* of the Hamiltonhill site also generated discussion. There was general acceptance of the fact that low-income, unskilled workers needed to be close to potential units of employment. But frequently, sites were simply not available in the areas of slum-clearance. It is therefore reasonable to assume that Hamiltonhill was the nearest available – and suitable – site to the Cowcaddens Clearance Area. The then and first Director of Housing, the energetic and innovative Peter Fyfe, specially mentioned this to the Inquiry into this Clearance Area:

> The difficulty of the Corporation is to get ground within a reasonable facility of those people who are going to be dispossessed . . . Half a mile is all the distance they should have to go, but in some cases the distance would be more than a mile. Personally, I am convinced that we are giving plenty of sunlight, skylight, and plenty of circulation of air, right round the buildings.

> If it could be proved otherwise, I would agree with any one against it, but I am satisfied that when you see them, you will satisfy yourself.[14]

Hamiltonhill was in fact 1.3 miles from the city centre (see map of schemes). The furthest that Cowcaddens tenants had to move to the new scheme was therefore just under a mile. But the huge Saracen ironworks and foundry were adjacent, and it is probable that a good number of Hamiltonhill men worked there as labourers. (Unfortunately the Saracen wage-books could not be traced.)

The Medical Officer of Health, Dr Chalmers, accepted that the house densities in Hamiltonhill were three times higher than those achieved in 1919 Act schemes. He also accepted that this constituted a liberal interpretation of the building regulations.[15] But this is hardly a valid comparison, since the Mosspark densities were extra-low, being achieved by building cottage-type houses. A more valid comparison would be with the 1919 Act Coplawhill Scheme, which contained tenements. There, the density was 26 houses per acre. Nevertheless, Corporation officials felt that they had done the best they could in their pioneering 'Rehousing' scheme at Hamiltonhill. Dr Chalmers was in no doubt about this:

> With regard to Hamiltonhill, I can say that there is an enormous improvement. It is simply not comparable.[16]

Tenanting

Remembering that Hamiltonhill was Glasgow's very first 'Slum-Clearance' scheme, the issue of a points system for prospective tenants of the type deployed in Mosspark was not an issue. The tenants in the slum-clearance areas like Muse Lane were simply informed that they were being rehoused, and ordered to move into the new scheme. But it is hardly surprising that the Corporation subjected its pioneer tenants to a battery of controls. After all, the Corporation had agonised over how to rehouse slum-dwellers from as early as 1892, the date of the first local housing Commission. Consequently Hamiltonhill – and all the other 'Rehousing' schemes in Glasgow – had a Resident Factor, who was responsible for the collection of rents and general supervision of tenants. This Factor was also responsible

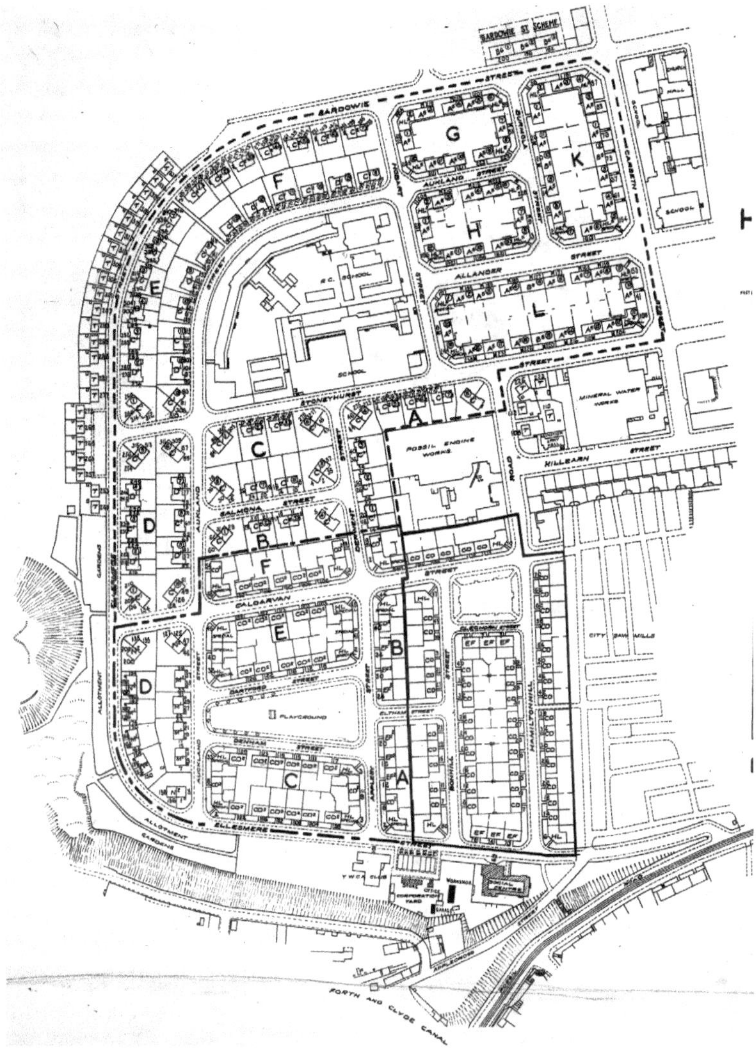

Figure 3.1 Hamiltonhill layout; Hamiltonhill is south of Stoneyhurst Street and west of Hamiltonhill Road

for the rent accounts, and for delivering the cash to Head Office. He was further responsible for repair and maintenance in the scheme, in that he reported complaints and faults to Building & Works. Finally, he had an important role in the maintenance of the moral order of the scheme as well as its physical appearance.

Figure 3.2 Hamiltonhill housing

The preferred background for these Resident Factors was tradesman, a practice adopted from the private factoring sector. Common sense and strength of personality were more important than formal educational qualifications. The Factors came into the Department through a variety of channels, including the Labour Exchange, but were all men of mature years. The job of a Resident Factor in the interwar years was an attractive proposition, for not only did it carry a reasonable wage, secure employment and a pension, but also a free house. The training of Resident Factors was strictly on the hoof; there was no formal training system. An outgoing Factor would explain his system and his tenants to the incumbent, often in a period of days. But obviously the Factors would discuss their work during their daily visits to Head Office. Finally, in both 'Intermediate' and 'Rehousing' schemes, the Resident Factor was a figure of very considerable authority, as will be demonstrated; he was respected but frequently not liked by tenants.

Tenants – particularly women – were also subject to supervision by a Public Health Nurse from the Public Health Department. She prefigured the later appointment of a 'Nurse Inspectress', with similar duties, by the Housing Department. Tenants frequently conflated the two as the ubiquitous

'Green Lady'. The duties of these Public Health Nurses (or inspectors) are summarised in a 1920 report:

> **Female Visitors**
> The duties of the female inspectors are to visit and instruct the poorer classes as to cleanliness of house, cleanliness of person, cleanliness of children, and cleanliness of bedding, to visit and examine children attending school, suspected of being infested with vermin, or in a filthy condition.[17]

These duties reflect the continuous obsession of the Corporation with the domestic dirtiness of slum tenants. Yet again, the problem was defined as the people who were forced to live in slums, as opposed to the slum-landlords who exploited rotten housing. So in what was actually called a 'sociological' experiment, the Corporation was determined to ensure that what it perceived as the engrained filthiness of slum-dwellers was not transferred to the prototype 'Slum-Clearance' scheme.[18] Hence, not only were its tenants patrolled, they were subject to prosecution for maintaining a dirty, that is, verminous, house, and the Corporation did not hesitate to prosecute. Such prosecutions as did take place were given maximum publicity by the local press.[19] Yet again, the focus is gendered. Women were perceived as having responsibility for the home, so the pressure was brought to bear on them, even though their husbands were the named tenants.

But of course, while the overt goal of the Corporation officials was to eradicate domestic dirtiness in the new council houses, the covert goal – and not very covert at that – was what Donzelot has called 'social hygiene'.[20] What is social hygiene? Donzelot provides an answer:

> Social hygiene is an economic science that has the human capital or material as its object, the latter's production or reproduction, its conservation, its utilisation, and its output. Social hygiene is a normative sociology: let us think of man as an industrial material, or more precisely as an animal machine. The hygienist is, then, the engineer of the human machine.[21]

The Hamiltonhill scheme was also provided with a Social Centre. This was to be the only purpose-built Centre in any of Glasgow's housing schemes. The only discussion I have been able to find of this Centre is

Figure 3.3 Hamiltonhill Social Centre

that it contained a Penny Savings Bank for tenants, aimed at meeting '. . . rent, clothes, footwear, and holidays'.[22] But given the historical attitude of the Corporation towards slum-dwellers, it is reasonable to assume that it was part of its general strategy of social hygiene. A subsequent – 1937 – extension to the Centre specifically included '. . . a demonstration kitchen and large occupational rooms for women, and a workshop provided for men'.[23] This provision stands in sharp contrast to the bowling greens, tennis courts and associated clubhouses of Mosspark and Riddrie, and was clearly gendered.

The occupational structure of the first tenants of Hamiltonhill reflects the marginal position of slum-dwellers in the local labour market. The Sub-Let Book (rental roll) for the scheme includes the following occupations: labourer, painter, craneman, locomotive shunter, billiard marker, joiner, bricklayer and carter.[24] Just over half, 52 per cent, were labourers (undefined); 16 per cent were involved in unskilled and semi-skilled work in the metal trades; 6 per cent were in the building trades; and 15 per cent were simply described as 'women' (see Occupational Structure table for details). This residual category must have included widows, including war widows; deserted wives; and what would now be called single-parent families. The Sub-Let Book describes several of these women as 'charwomen'. In any event, the original occupational structure of Hamiltonhill reflected that of the Cowcaddens slums whence came the first tenants, and permits us to see that single women were particularly vulnerable in both the housing and labour markets. (And that is why there were 'model' lodging-houses for women as well as men in Victorian Glasgow.) The changes in the tenancy structure of the scheme are presented in the Table at the end of the chapter.

Pioneer Tenants

The few remaining original tenants in Hamiltonhill at the time of the research were, of course, children at the time of the move. Many of these original tenants came from big families in the slums of the Cowcaddens. One elderly tenant came in 1923 as a three-year-old from the horrific Muse Lane, discussed earlier:

> Mr F: There were six children in the family.

And:

> Mrs N: Well there were thirteen of us.
>
> SD: Thirteen children?
>
> Mrs N: Uh huh . . . there was a woman who stayed in Denham Street and she was in a room-and-kitchen. Now do you remember the *Citizen* newspaper? An evening paper it was. She was in the *Evening Citizen* and she had twenty-one children in a room-and-kitchen in the scheme. They nick-named her Black Mary.

The actual move is remembered:

> Mrs B: One lorry took our flitting. It was a horse and cart thing. That took our flitting. There were no fancy motors or anything like that in these days.

And:

> Mrs L: Aye, we came in a horse and cart. I can remember it. It was the 29th December. It was two days before Hogmanay.

The new house was greeted with universal joy:

> Mrs C: Oh I couldn't describe the joy it was to see the hoose and the white wood floors . . . It was really a good feeling.

And:

> Mrs N: It was great, my goodness the size of it alone, you know. It was great. Then my father, he – I always remember his saying to my mother, 'Leave the gas on a peep for the older sisters coming.'
>
> SD: What else struck you as being interesting?
>
> Mrs N: Well, the bath, you know, and the inside toilet.

Glaswegian tenants always remarked on the sheer size of their new council houses as compared with the grotesque overcrowding in the slums, and their joy at an inside toilet – plus a bath!

But the only thing in the scheme that was finished was the houses:

> Mrs N: When we came up here first there were nae pavements. The front gardens and the back greens were all mud. I mean they werenae sorted oot because they were still building. They were still making pavements. As I said, we had to walk up a plank of wood to get into the close. So the work was still going on.

This unfinished situation was also common in postwar schemes. There wasn't a lot of money about:

> Mrs N: Well, as I says, my father worked as an outside labourer. Now as you know, when it rained and your father lost time, he never was paid. I always used to hear my mother say, 'I hope to God it doesn't rain today and you can get a couple of hours in, Jimmy.' Now at that time I am talking about I think it was only about a shilling or so an hour he got paid and if he was laid off with the rain for six hours, six shillings he lost that day, that kind of thing. If it was raining he got knocked off and he didn't get paid for it.

And:

> Mrs N: To be truthful, we didnae have much furniture, you know. A wardrobe, well you didnae have the clothes to put in a wardrobe and I was the

> one who was always getting the hand-me-downs from my sisters. But we had our beds and then in the living-room we had a table, what they call a kitchen-table and my mother used to scrub it white, the bed and the sideboard, a rocking-chair and an ordinary chair and then a couple more chairs. So it was hard to furnish.

The women made 'patch-mats' for the beds:

> Mrs N: There would be one blanket and two patch-mats with old bits of cloth all sewed thegither on two sides and maybe there was an old blanket put in the centre and sewed up, that is what they called a patch-mat. We will say for instance that you had three or four old frocks. You cut them up and made square sheets, patched two of them and then maybe an old torn blanket, you know, worn blankets, they would go in the centre and you would stitch it roon and doon the centre and that was your patch-mat.

In fact, there was a market in the scheme for both patch-mats and shawls made by local women, and while Ann McGuckin has described this whole process well, the sheer ingenuity of these women in making money go further, and adapting what they could get their hands on, is seriously underestimated in the academic literature.[25]

Some of this local economy was organised in menages. Menage, pronounced 'menodge', is a Scots word deriving from the French *ménage*. It refers to a small-scale local savings club to which each member – usually women – contributes a small weekly sum.

> Mrs N: Well I'm going back before the war and there was a wee woman and she is dead noo and she stayed in Appleby Street. I was a great knitter when I was young and I crocheted. Now I had an auntie of my mother's and I met her with my mother one day and she had a lovely crocheted shawl on and I was standing near the shawl and I says, I am going to have a go at that. Now I crocheted a red one and my mother said, where did you get the idea for that? I says, just from my Auntie Pat so I thought I would thingummy it. So she said, I'll get you the wool and can dae me one. I said, you can take that one. So I done my mother a blue one, and then it got round. So this woman in Appleby Street she run a menage

for the shawls that I crocheted. I would maybe crotchet two a week, it depended, but there was about two and a half pound of wool in it and I used to go to Paisley. I did quite a few of the crocheted shawls in Hamiltonhill.

SD: So how much would you get for a shawl?

Mrs N: Five shillings.

SD: Only five shillings?

Mrs N: But that was a lot of money then when I am talking aboot.

SD: But still and all, ten shillings for two shawls for a week's work?

Mrs N: But it was still a lot of money for the likes of us because my man was working and his wages was 35/-. Well if you use 30/- to run the hoose and you have to dae everything with it and save for holidays and that, you were glad of the extra 10/-.

Another survival mechanism involved using the services of a tenant who had an account with the Co-op. Basically the idea was that this person would get goods on account for a neighbour, and the latter would pay up in instalments. The benefit to the account-holder was that she got the dividend – 2/- in the pound – on this purchase:

Mr P: My wife is the account-holder and I came along and say, look here, wee Jimmy needs an outfit because he is going to school today. She would then authorise to go to the Co-op and charge her account. I would then pay, say it was £20 I would then pay her up to that amount of £20. Where she would get the benefit, she would get her dividend at 2/- in the pound. She would get the monetary value. So in effect it was a service without bleeding the public not like today as the sharks that we know at the present day you never get out of the debt. Here was a scheme that somebody had devised that you paid the account because they were in that position and you paid it up and they allowed you to pay it up.

Again, this is a highly inventive coping strategy, but one which indicates that Hamiltonhill was not totally homogenous, as membership of the Co-op was very much for 'respectable' working-class women.

Simple, non-violent money-lending for modest amounts of interest existed in the scheme, with one family being principally involved.

> Mrs O'D: Well, across the road there the daughter still lives, and the brother and I palled it wi' their younger sister. So this Mrs Brown would say to me, Betty, going to go to Mrs Finlay and get a loan of a wee half-crown. My mother nearly took a fit when she found out because she said if she was short of money she would rather go to a pawn than that. So anyway, Mrs M would make me jump the railings and go up to her house and get a loan of a half-a-crown for her, and then she had to pay so much back in interest. She was the only one that I knew.

And:

> Mr P: There was never any violence and there was never anybody that would go and threaten so-and-so for not paying; that didn't happen.

But life was not all coping mechanisms; all the traditional children's games and pranks raged in Hamiltonhill.

> Mrs N: We used to have a game when we were young which was to tie two bottom doors together, chap the door and run away. Now whoever's door it was if they spotted you, I knew the next day when I came in from school the way I got pulled in as soon as the door was opened and my mother was there and I got battered. It was efter she battered me she would say to me, do you know what this is for? That is for tying Mrs so-and-so's door. She must have seen me and told my mother. They were the kind of things that you were up against. The people then, their kids were chastised but they weren't as cheeky as they are noo.

And:

> Mr P: They played skipping ropes, this kind of thing. I am talking about the adults and I remember quite well. They had played rounders and actually their parents were involved with the families in these days. They would go out there and play at rounders and this sort of stuff and skipping ropes. Again as I say in these days there were a lot of Picture Halls in and around this area and the idea was to take the children to the matinees on a Tuesday and a Thursday. I remember quite well on a Tuesday getting two pence and that was a penny to get me into the Picture Hall and a penny to get me sweeties, buttermilk Dainties, and that was an every

> week thing. In this area you had the Possil Picture House which was in Saracen Street. You had the Astoria Picture Hall which was just down at County Bingo that you see just now. You were only yards from a Magnet Picture Hall.

And the boys were Glasgow boys:

> Mr P: When I was a wee boy it was fitba. That was wir life – my life. I could play from morning to night, till dark time and they would be shouting at you to come into the house. That was my life, nothing else. Football all the time.

The degree of internal social organisation – sometimes called 'community spirit' – in Hamiltonhill is evidenced by the sheer number of football teams produced in this small scheme.

> SD: What kind of thing used to go on in that Social Centre?
>
> Mr P: Well first of all they had the football team, the Hamiltonhill Social, they were a great team. In fact, they won seven cups and the shield in one year.
>
> SD: Were there any kids' teams?
>
> Mr P: Aye, well we had the Midgets. We had the Midget fitba doon in the square doon past Willy's. I was a footballer myself. We had the Hamiltonhill Midgets, that was us. Then we had the Oatland Star up at the top of the street. There was another wee man who ran the Kildoran Star. We played all sorts of teams from Anderston. We used to go down to Anderston to play, Whitehill Street, and Anderston Cambridge came up to play us up here.
>
> SD: So in the years before the war the scheme was supporting three Junior Football teams?
>
> Mr P: Well we were secondary, junior, juvenile, you know.
>
> SD: So there were three juvenile teams and a junior team. So there were four football teams coming out of this scheme?
>
> Mr P: Aye.
>
> SD: Three teams of kids and one team of young men?
>
> Mr P: Aye.
>
> SD: That's pretty good for a small scheme?

> Mr P: When the Midgets would play this place was chock-a-block with them. They were oot of their windaes and that, and went roon with the hat and that got us oor fitba strips and boots and things like that.

The sheer ebullience of children's play and football in Hamiltonhill reminds us that working-class children play in the street, and provides a sharp cultural comparison with the repressed situation in Mosspark where children were to be neither seen nor heard.

The public nature of working-class culture in Hamiltonhill is also evidenced by the fact that back-court buskers were also common.

> Mr H: The buskers used to come to the back court with their accordion on a Sunday morning. They would play one tune and as soon as you threw the penny they would go away anyway.

And:

> Mrs T: Yes every Saturday they came round.
>
> SD: Who came round?
>
> Mrs T: Men playing the accordion and singing. Well one would play the accordion and the other would sing. We would then open the windae, well my mother did and throw them over money.

For all the scheme contained a vibrant street life, the tenants were still officially 'slum-clearees' and therefore subject to rigid supervision by Corporation officials.

> Mrs N: Our first factor was in Hamiltonhill Road and he was an elderly man, a wee stout man. In fact he would walk aboot the scheme at ten o'clock at night to watch everybody going up and doon and if he saw a stranger going up a close he would chap the door and ask, who was that that came in? And was he staying there? And if he was staying there you had to get him oot.

And:

> Mrs L: The factor would just go up and chap your door and say, listen, it is time that you washed those windows and stairs. They would also walk at night and make sure and say, there is Mary Napier going up, eh, who is

> that is wi her? That is no her man. He could tell. He would want to know if that was a lodger or no.

What the factor was looking for were tenants living in houses on illegal sub-lets, but it is noteworthy that the tenants did not seem to object to such authoritarian treatment. They had been used to it since mid-Victorian times.

> SD: What kind of guy was this factor?
>
> Mr P: Oh he was quite a good chap, quite a good fellow. Especially he wouldn't allow anything happening in the scheme. He kept going on roon aboot all the time.
>
> SD: What was he looking out for?
>
> Mr P: Well even with boys playing in the street with a ball and that, playing football and that he didnae agree with that in case the windaes getting broken and that. In fact I have even seen him catching the ball and taking it aff them. He was a good factor that way.

What the Resident Factor was trying to do was to reinforce the notion of 'respectability'. If Hamiltonhill was a 'good' scheme where children did not play on the streets, and tenants did not sub-let, then they were by definition 'good people'.

The dreaded 'Green Lady' – named after her uniform – was also much in evidence.

> Mrs N: We had a woman and she was called Buggy Annie. She was a sanitary woman. It is a sad fact that they have done away with her because they could do with her back. Now she would come up every six weeks and inspect your house. She knew houses that she had to inspect. She even looked at your bed. She would go into a house that she knew was clean and she would just look around and that was it. But if she went into a house that wisnae just . . . she went round all the house and she would soon tell you that you have got so long to get that clean and so long to get that clean.

And:

> Mrs O'D: They lifted your bed clothes and your bedding to make sure there wis no fleas or bugs or anything like that. To see if it was clean. They could go into anything in your house and look.

SD: And how often did these Green Ladies come round?

Mrs O'D: You never knew. They just came round about once a month. Oh aye, if they were kinda wary of somebody's house they would just pounce on them.

These interviews were conducted in 1990, and suggest that the respondents believed there was evidence of 'slipping standards' of social behaviour in council housing. Hence their somewhat rose-tinted recall of the more authoritarian era of their younger days. In the 1990s, and now, tenants would simply not put with such invasive behaviour. But in the 1920s and 1930s, in housing schemes like Hamiltonhill, such moral policing was accepted normality, and constituted a direct continuation of the midnight raids of the sanitary inspectors on ticketed houses.

The Police, of course, were also in evidence.

Mr H: Yes, they had in these days the beat policeman. He would come around – and they are trying to bring it back. There would be a beat cop and he would just patrol the area and he would get to know the neighbours. He would get information without even asking and so-and-so wasn't doing what he should have been doing or whatever. He was a respected individual too. Again in these days if it was warranted he would give you a clout across the ear for whatever, and you daren't go in and say to your parents that a policeman struck me because you would get another for that, so if you got one belt across the ear you were certainly not going to get two.

But the Police were concerned with criminal behaviour. The City Improvements Department was still responsible for issues to do with the payment, or non-payment, of rent. Although the missive for the rent was monthly, it was actually paid weekly; the tenants could not afford to pay monthly:

Mrs N: The rents were paid weekly because you couldn't afford to leave it for a month. It was too much. It was 28/-. If you had left it you would never have made it up, so it was paid weekly.

There was the odd eviction:

Mrs L: I can remember an eviction. They stayed two closes up and it was a Saturday and it was that man McKenna [real name] who went down to the Court for her and he came back. Well all her stuff was in the close and then he says, come on, that's it, you are evicted from here and that was a three-apartment. So he took her and put her into a two-apartment. McKenna got her sorted out with the arrears.

As the Depression wore on, more tenants were evicted for rent arrears. This led to a formal Question in the Corporation.

2.2.28: Councillor Forgan to the Convenor of the Housing Committee.

Will the Committee state:-

(1) The number of cases up-to-date in which Hamiltonhill rehousing scheme tenants have been ejected for non-payment of rent or other reason; and

(2) The number of vacancies thus created which have been filled by tenants selected from the over-crowded and insanitary conditions of Woodside Ward?[26]

However, the man McKenna quoted by Mrs L above alerts us to the fact that there were active Socialist politics in Hamiltonhill. Mr McKenna was in fact a Communist. There were others:

Mrs F: And we had three men up here and I remember that they went to the Spanish Civil War and they were killed in it.

SD: Can you remember their names?

Mrs F: McDade, McQuade and McMorrow. I can always remember that they went to war.

SD: So were these men Socialists or Communists? They must have been.

Mrs F: Communists.

Alex McDade was indeed a Communist, and is famous for writing the haunting song about the International Brigade, *There's a Valley in Spain Called Jarama.*

And:

SD: What about politics? Did you have any politics?

Mr H: Yes. We were very much involved in Labour. My father and my uncle and he was a Councillor back in these early days. Very much involved in Labour.

So Hamiltonhill was as naturally a left-wing scheme as Mosspark was right-wing, in political terms. Interestingly, early tenants state emphatically that the vicious sectarianism which characterised other parts of Glasgow was absent in Hamiltonhill.

Mrs F: It was a mixed scheme, so it wis. I mean when we were young, okay, what do they call the Catholics? The Micks, and we were the Proddy dogs, you know, but, we didnae fight over them. In fact, I married a Catholic. And that has never once been brought up in the forty-odd years that we have been married.

And:

SD: Would you say that this was a more Catholic scheme or a Protestant scheme?

Mrs B: Catholic.

Mr B: I would say it was more a Catholic scheme. In fact, they used to cry it 'Little Ireland'.

Mrs B: I think all the Catholics came from Cowcaddens.

SD: Was there ever any trouble within the scheme or outside the scheme between Catholics and Protestants? I mean, in the Orange type of thing?

Mr B: No, naw, we never had arguments with them.

Mrs B: There were only two Protestants and four Catholics up this close and there was never an angry word. My mother was one of these women who used to dye her curtains orange for the 12th of July and put them up. The woman in the close dyed hers green for the 17th of March. There was never any aggro. They just always done it. They worked together in Bilsland's Bread Works in Finnieston Street. It is in Anderston and my mother had the orange strand ribbons in her hair on the 12th of July and her pal she was a Catholic and she had the green in her hair on the 17th of March and they were the best of pals.

And:

SD: So on the 12th, for example, there wouldn't be any . . . ?

Mrs N: No, no. You never ever seen . . . The only thing maybe they would hiv up the blue curtains on the 12th of July and the Catholics would have up green curtains. There wis never any dispute, no. You never got any fighting about it.

It might be felt, reasonably enough, that these tenants were downplaying sectarianism, but I heard similar comments often enough to believe that solidarity in the face of poverty overcame religious differences. Indeed, there was a great deal of community self-help and mutual services in Hamiltonhill, mainly organised by women. This was necessary because no one else was providing the required services – so the local women did it themselves.

Mrs N: There were many people that went and did their midwife because in they days they didnae have the money sometimes to pay the midwife and them went out and helped. The only thing wis if it was going to be dangerous the doctor would be sent for. That is the only thing. But there wis many a one helped out.

And:

Mr G: There was my grandmother who again like my wife's mother was never educated but she had this facility and skill and God's gift if you like to be a midwife, untrained. She was called upon on many occasions during the war because we had one doctor, it was Dr MacRae and he was always overloaded. He would call her in the early hours of the morning to go, and I as a boy had to get up in the early hours of the morning, get my torch because it was the blackout days, and go round to whoever was having a child. My grandmother got a lot of people, births, into this area. She was known and she had this gift.

The diseases associated with poverty were well known:

> LH: Were there any other cases of TB in the scheme?
>
> Mrs P: No.
>
> Mr P: Yes, *in* the scheme.
>
> Mrs P: Oh aye, in the scheme.
>
> Mr P: TB and again TB in these days was a horrible thing and if somebody had TB you wanted to . . . I am glad to say that people have been educated and these things don't happen. But in these days it did and it was quite a . . .

And:

> Mrs M: I lost a brother with TB but he was nineteen years of age. It was through . . . He took pneumonia and he went back to work too soon.
>
> SD: How old were you when this happened?
>
> Mr M: You would be eighteen or nineteen.
>
> Mrs M: I was in Ruchill [Hospital] and I can always remember the nurse saying to my Ma, well if you take your girl home she won't last.
>
> SD: Was this TB?
>
> Mr M: Yes.

And:

> SD: Was there any TB about the scheme?
>
> Mrs H: Oh aye. Quite a lot of TB. In fact, there were two or three in the one family died with it. Rheumatic Fever and that.

And:

> Mrs N: There was an awful lot of young ones up here died with Tuberculosis. There was one family and it was just after the war started there was two of them buried, a son and daughter. Across from where I stayed there wis another two, one was Meningitis and the other was Tuberculosis. There was a lot of that going about then.

However, besides disease, there were other, environmental, dangers for local children:

Mrs F: The big bogey here was the canal. We were always told not to go near the canal. Two or three of the kids did lose their lives in it – in the canal. You see, the sawmill used to use the canal to mature the wood and they had these big boxes of timber in it. Well if they were from end to end they would run across them.

And:

Mrs N: I will tell you something else, quite a few kids from the scheme got drowned in the canal. I know up here I can remember four or five boys were drowned in the canal.

In spite of the poverty, unemployment and related illness, and the small size of the houses, Hamiltonhill in the first two or three decades of its existence was perceived by its tenants as an excellent housing scheme. In their testimony, Glasgow Corporation's prototype 'Slum-Clearance' scheme was an outstanding success:

Mrs N: I think it was quite a good place to live. I always liked Hamiltonhill.
SD: A friendly place?
Mrs N: Very friendly. You don't get the same friendliness now among the neighbours that we had then. But then when we stayed here and if my neighbour was short of a shilling and I had a shilling I would lend it to her. If I am short I could go to my neighbour. It was that kind of atmosphere. It wisnae a kind of greedy place, it wisnae an envious place then as it is now.

And:

Mr R: I would say marvellous people. I can't say nothing against any of them.
SD: It sounds like you two people were happy in your life here anyway?
Mr R: Aye, aye.
Mrs R: Very happy.

And:

Mr M: Hamiltonhill people – they are always very proud. I would say that Hamiltonhill would probably be like a very close community.

> Neighbours helped each other in every respect and I just highlighted it earlier as I mentioned about my grandmother being a midwife and the like – it is a good community spirit.

Oddly enough, Hamiltonhill, perhaps because of its small size and relatively hidden location, remained unknown to Glasgow at large. In this sense, it happily escaped the stigma which Blackhill had to endure for more than four decades, as will be demonstrated shortly.

> Mrs T: Naw it's not everybody who knew Hamiltonhill, funnily enough, even to this day. No many people know. We have got a taxi . . . look at that night we got a taxi from Saracen and he said, 'You'll need to tell me how to get into it.' I said, 'Don't tell me you don't know Hamiltonhill?' Aye, no many people know where Hamiltonhill is even to this day.

Summary

Glasgow's prototype 'Slum-Clearance' scheme experienced several major problems – or, more correctly, its tenants experienced them. These were poverty, TB, irregular employment or unemployment, and a dangerous location near the Forth & Clyde Canal. And the two-apartment houses were too small for the big families from the slums. Indeed, by 1930 the City Improvements Department estimated that 51 per cent of houses in the scheme were overcrowded.[27] That said, the pioneer tenants of Hamiltonhill adapted the traditional working-class survival culture of the slum tenements successfully into a pattern which made their new scheme into a cheerful and happy if overcrowded community. It is hardly surprising that the tenants appreciated their new houses as much as they did, for the municipal tenements in the interwar and postwar schemes were a vast improvement on traditional privately owned tenements. Not only had the Corporation taken the initiative in experimenting with building materials,[28] but also the municipal tenements were better built and equipped, and population densities were much lower.

Hamiltonhill was an overwhelmingly manual working-class scheme, and unskilled manual at that. Its population was very stable up until the Second World War, with just over half of its population being classed as 'labourers'. But there was some increase in skilled manual workers throughout the 1930s and war years. The biggest change occurred after the war, when the proportion of women tenants increased to 35 per cent in 1948. This 200 per cent-plus increase was probably due to an informal policy of perceiving the small houses in Hamiltonhill as suitable for working-class single-parent families headed by women, on the one hand, and an accretion of war widows on the other. In any event, in terms of rehousing slum-dwellers satisfactorily, Hamiltonhill was a successful experiment for all but a tiny minority of its original tenants.

So well before the passage of the 1930 Housing Act, Glasgow Corporation had tackled its housing problem at both the top and bottom ends of the market. While this was greatly to its credit, the fact of the matter was that the 'general needs' of the working class had not yet even been touched.

Table 3.1 Hamiltonhill occupational structure, 1925–1948

% by column	1925	1935	1948
Skilled manual	6	15	13
Semi-skilled manual	16	6	5
Unskilled manual	63	66	47
Women	15	13	35

Notes

NB: All references preceded by 'GCA' refer to the Glasgow City Archives.

1. Bowley (1947) and Merrett (1979), op. cit.
2. *Corporation Minutes*, Joint Sub-Committee on Slum Areas, Print No. 12, p. 1192, 21 March 1922.
3. *Glasgow Herald*, 7 July 1922.
4. Glasgow Corporation Housing Department, *Review of Operations 1919–1937*, pp. 25–6.
5. GCA D-TC7/12/2/1: Glasgow Corporation Housing Department: *Review of Operations 1919–1927*, p. 18.
6. Sir Alexander Macgregor (1967): *Public Health in Glasgow, 1905–1937*, E. & S. Livingstone, p. 50.
7. GCA D-HE/4/1/7/1 – Housing (Scotland) Act 1925: The Glasgow Improvement Scheme 1926: Report of Proceedings at Inquiry.
8. Ibid., paras 26, 38.
9. Ibid., para. 38.

10. *Glasgow Herald*, 28 March 1924, p. 6.
11. Glasgow Corporation Housing Department, *Review of Operations 1919–1927*, op. cit.
12. GCA, *Questions to the Corporation*, Vol. 4, 1923.
13. *Corporation Minutes*, Print No. 13, p. 1201, 30 March 1922.
14. *Report* (1923), op. cit., paras 1308–9.
15. Ibid., para. 1237.
16. Ibid., para. 777.
17. GCA D-HE/1/4/16: *Mss. Report from Divisional Sanitary Inspector No. 5 Division*, February 1920.
18. Cf. Chalmers (ed.) (1905); *Annual Report Glasgow M.O.H. 1929.*
19. For concrete examples of such prosecution and publicity in Govan in the 1930s, see Damer (1989), pp. 110ff.
20. Donzelot, J. (1979), *The Policing of Families: Welfare Versus the State*, Hutchinson.
21. Ibid., p. 186, quoted in Damer (2000), op. cit., p. 2012.
22. GCA D-TC6/606/5/10.
23. Corporation of Glasgow Housing Department, *Review of Operations 1919–1937*, p. 12.
24. GCA D-CF3/7.
25. McGuckin, A. (1922), 'Moving Stories: Working-Class Women', in E. Breitenbach and E. Gordon (eds), *Out of Bounds: Women in Scottish Society 1800–1945*, Edinburgh University Press, pp. 197ff.
26. GCA, *Questions to the Corporation*, Book No. 5, 1928.
27. GCA D-HE/5/3/17: Housing Notes: 'Overcrowding in Corporation Houses', p. 3.
28. This experimentation is detailed in Morgan, N. (1989), '"£8 cottages for Glasgow citizens": Innovations in municipal house-building in Glasgow in the inter-war years', in R. Rodger (ed.), *Scottish Housing in the Twentieth Century*, Leicester University Press.

4

West Drumoyne: Blue-Collarland

The Legislation

West Drumoyne was built under the provisions of John Wheatley's 1924 Housing Act. This Act re-introduced the principle of state subsidy of council housing, and was aimed squarely at those 'general needs' of the working class totally untouched by the 1919 Act. Its provisions ensured the acceleration of the house-building programme both nationally and in Glasgow. But even with design criteria markedly less generous that those of the 1919 Act, the nature of the rigid subsidy system resulted in rent levels which were still out of reach of the majority of workers.

The problem which not even Wheatley had resolved was a differential rent policy, that is, an economic strategy for constructing adequate houses at rents which the different sections of the working class could afford. The old question of not being seen to subsidise the rents of the poor out of the rents of more affluent remained unanswered. In Glasgow, the council housing which had been constructed by the mid-1920s was élite housing for professionals, white-collar workers and the odd labour aristocrat on the one hand, and a very small amount of basic housing for slum-dwellers on the other. This still left unresolved the problem of how to house the intermediate – and by far the largest – category of tenant: the mass of workers housed in overcrowded tenements which were not technical slums. At this late date, 1924, and indeed until 1928, there was no such thing as 'Intermediate' council housing in Glasgow. The failure of government legislation to meet the housing needs of these workers resulted in considerable agitation in Glasgow on the part of the ILP for a category of scheme midway between the low rentals of designated 'Slum-Clearance' schemes like Hamiltonhill, and the very much higher rents in 'Ordinary' schemes like Mosspark.

The outcome was the conscious creation of a new, third, category of housing scheme, the 'Intermediate'. The first of these schemes were subsidised under the Wheatley Act, others under subsequent interwar legislation. Other local authorities solved the problem through a differential rents policy, thus maintaining a two-tier system. This, of course, meant that ratepayers and better-off tenants of council housing schemes were subsidising those on lower rents.

In Glasgow, the ruling political party was the Moderates, a Tory–Liberal coalition with the former being very much the dominant faction. But in the climate of the time, the Moderates had to be seen to be supporting council housing, and indeed had their own housing experts like Councillors Morton and Steel. Their political problem was how to pay for council housing. The population of Glasgow requiring 'Intermediate' housing was so large that a differential rent system would have meant political suicide. Hence, the Moderates and the ILP were in agreement that a quite separate category of council housing scheme was required. The political difference lay in the type of houses which were to be erected in these schemes, and the attendant rent structure. The battle was fought out over West Drumoyne.

Site Development

In 1928 Glasgow Corporation bought 42 acres of agricultural land at West Drumoyne for £24,500.[1] But within the Corporation there was fierce political conflict on how to develop this site. The ILP plan, proposed by Councillor Mary Barbour of Govan, a veteran leader of the 1915 Glasgow Rent Strike, was 84 cottage houses, 272 flats (four-in-a-block) and 384 three-storey tenements, with an overall density of 16.63 houses per acre. Thus the ILP's proposal for this prototype 'Intermediate' scheme was that they should maintain the imaginative mix of housing built under the 1919 Act for 'Ordinary' schemes, but with 'Intermediate' rents. In other words, the ILP wanted the same good housing mix for ordinary blue-collar workers as had been provided for the salariat of Mosspark.

But this proposal was countered by two others. The first involved 200 flats and 798 three-storey tenements, at a density of 22.43 houses per acre.

This was proposed by Bailie Swan, seconded by Councillor William Smith, both from the Moderate Party.[2] The second involved 1,212 three-storey tenements with a density of 27.32 houses per acre proposed by Councillor Logie, Convenor of the Housing Committee, seconded by Bailie McCluskey, again both Moderates. These competing plans generated considerable heat within the Corporation. The ILP's proposals were passed by the Sub-Committee on Sites and Buildings. At the full Housing Committee, the Moderates objected strenuously but were defeated on the vote. However, the full council, which was controlled by the Moderates, overturned Mary Barbour's plan. But matters did not end here; the proposals were again referred to the Sub-Committee and the debate raged on throughout 1929.

An amended layout of 810 houses in three-storey tenements and 60 in two-storey tenements, at a density of 26.29 houses per acre, was finally passed.[3] This represented a considerable defeat for the radical proposals of the ILP, and the class polarisation was now clearly evident. However, the affair was far from over. In March 1930 the Scottish Board of Health objected in detail to this proposal when it was forwarded to it for approval. The Board said:

> There was submitted a letter from the Department of Health of Scotland stating that the Department's Chief Architect considers it inadvisable to approve three-storey tenements in close proximity to the existing schemes at Shieldhall, Greenhead and Drumoyne which are composed of cottages and two-storey flatted houses and that it would be regrettable if the proposed tenemental development were adhered to particularly as the site is of an open nature. It is desirable from a Town Planning point of view to preserve the amenity of the schemes already built. It is suggested that the section of houses to the West of the site facing Moss Road should be of the two-storey flatted type and that the section facing Shieldhall be of the two-storey flatted variety also or two-storey tenements and that if the Corporation so desire that the houses in the centre and South of the site might be of the three-storey tenement type. However, it is advisable that there should be a gradual approach from the two-storey cottages in the adjoining Shieldhall Scheme to the three-storey tenements on the Southside of the West Drumoyne Scheme.[4]

The following month, the *Glasgow Herald* printed a story suggesting dirty work at the crossroads.[5] The Master of Works was accused of trying to sabotage the tenemental layout approved for West Drumoyne by the Corporation in that he went personally to the Scottish Board of Health to make representations. There was a curious similarity, said Councillor Logie (Mod.), Convenor of the Housing Committee, between the suggestions of the Master of Works and those of the Board.

A most important political principle was being debated here. The ILP wanted 'Ordinary' grade houses for its constituents at 'Intermediate' rents, on the basis that if it's good enough for the middle class, it's good enough for us. This was anathema to the Moderates, particularly the Tories among them, for self-evidently they were more 'deserving' than mere workers. The Scottish Board of Health could afford to adopt a Pontius Pilate attitude to whatever kind of housing went up in West Drumoyne as the existing legislation meant that ratepayers and better-off council tenants would inevitably subsidise such 'Intermediate' rents. Local Govanites also expressed disquiet at the proposed design of the West Drumoyne houses. Their objections, however, would appear to be motivated by self-interest rather than political principle, signifying important distinctions within the working class. Their letters to the local newspaper are given below.

> Sir
> Allow me through your columns to express indignation at the Town Council's decision to build tenement houses in Drumoyne West. Have we not sufficient of these barracks in our city already? I can well understand Councillor T. A. Kerr expressing himself freely when he sees 'dove-cots' in the form of tenements being built on what will become in the near future a part of a garden city. Electors of Fairfield Ward see to it that Councillor Kerr gets full support and banish this type of house which had been a blot in our city.
> I am etc.
> Cruachan.[6]

And:

> Sir
> In the last week's issue of the Press your correspondent Cruachan has expressed the feelings of the tenants of Drumoyne, Greenhead and Shieldhall and if the facts were known, the whole of the city. Who in Glasgow does not want his door and garden? The days of potential rookeries are past. The Department of Health for Scotland has acknowledged this fact in the recommendation regarding the Drumoyne West Scheme. Councillor T. A. Kerr has voiced his opinion in this direction and it is up to the electorate of the city to give him full support.
> I am etc.
> Tartan.[7]

It is clear that both 'Cruachan' and 'Tartan' see themselves as 'superior' residents of the 'Ordinary' schemes of Drumoyne, Shieldhall or Greenhead, in the vicinity. The issue here is that, by 1930, new council *tenemental* schemes were invariably associated with 'Slum-Clearance'/'Rehousing' schemes, thus displaying a public stigma. This reflected a deeply held but erroneous belief in the ranks of organised labour in Glasgow that as all slums were tenements, all working-class tenements were therefore slums – a fallacy that persisted until well after the Second World War.

In any event, the final plan for the scheme *was* tenemental. Its final density was again contested between the Corporation and the Scottish Board of Health. When the final plan was approved in 1931, it was for 732 tenement houses of three storeys, with the blocks facing Shieldhall Road being two-storey. A year later, an extension of 104 houses was approved. The final house mix was 68 three-apartment and 150 four-apartment houses. As opposed to the situation in subsequent 'Rehousing' schemes, there were no two-apartment houses. An anomaly within this scheme was the construction of 57 four-in-a-block houses just north of Shieldhall Road, adjacent to the 'Ordinary' scheme of Drumoyne. A not unreasonable conclusion is that this small enclave of flatted houses was constructed as a sop to the finer feelings of the tenants of Drumoyne. In other words, considerations of social class, masquerading as Town Planning, can be seen to have had a direct effect on council housing construction and layout policy in this scheme.

Tenanting

The 732 houses in 11 sections in West Drumoyne were completed by the first half of 1933, although letting began in June 1932. Almost all, nearly 90 per cent, of the first tenants of West Drumoyne came from the old shipbuilding and engineering neighbourhoods in its immediate vicinity, in the south-west of the city: Linthouse, Govan, Kinning Park, Plantation and Kingston. Eighty-one per cent were skilled or semi-skilled workers, reflecting accurately the fact that the engineering and shipbuilding industries in Glasgow were top-heavy in skill terms. Of the tenants, 226 (27 per cent) worked in the Govan Shipyards – Stephen's of Linthouse, Fairfield, Harland & Wolff. A small number, 29, worked in identifiable local engineering works, and 88 (roughly 1 in 10) were Corporation workers, principally in transport. Twenty-seven worked in the Clyde Navigation Trust, while forty-six worked in the Co-op at Shieldhall. Thus, West Drumoyne was a resolutely blue-collar housing scheme, containing a representative mix of the classic south-west Glasgow industrial occupations. (Typically, a blue-collar worker is an urban, industrial person involved in manual labour which may be skilled or unskilled, often where something is physically being constructed or maintained.) The 'general needs' of the local working class were at last beginning to be met, 13 years after the first government initiative.

There are two points about the above data. Firstly, they are derived from the Draft Rolls and Valuation Rolls. There is no way of discerning in these sources whether or not a tenant was working. The period 1930–5 saw the height of the Depression in Glasgow; it was a period when there was never less than 25 per cent of all insured male workers unemployed, while many other men were working short time. Secondly, 22 (22.6 per cent) of the scheme's original tenants were registered as 'women', 'widows' or 'domestic duties'. Many of these women must have been single parents. The point is that such women were perceived as legitimate tenants of 'Intermediate' houses. The proportion of women tenants was to increase dramatically between 1938 and 1948. This increase can probably be accounted for by a growing number of widows whose husbands, the original tenants, had died, or had been killed in the war. These single women were accepted as tenants, thus saving them from homelessness and destitution. The ILP deserves great credit for this important innovation, and it is not hard to discern the hands of Socialist activists like Mary Barbour and Helen Crawfurd of the South Govan Housing Association in it.

The housing background of the original tenants is verified by their grown-up sons' and daughters' oral testimony. Some make the point that the tenemental houses in which they lived in Govan were reasonable; by-and-large they were not slums. They were the small and hence overcrowded tenement houses which formed the biggest single proportion of Glasgow's housing:

> SD: That house in Howat Street – what kind of house was it?
>
> Mr R: A room and kitchen.
>
> SD: An outside toilet or an inside toilet?
>
> Mr R: I think it did have an inside toilet. It was classified as one of the better areas in Govan.

And:

> SD: In Greenfield Street what kind of house was that?
>
> Mr G: It was a through room-and-kitchen with inside toilet.
>
> SD: That would be considered a good house?
>
> Mr G: To me it was a good house.

The point here is, as the Blackhill data will demonstrate, 'Rehousing' schemes were full of slum-dwellers who were under no illusion that they *had* lived in slums. But the original tenants of the 'Intermediate' schemes tended to come from reasonable, if small and overcrowded, tenement houses.

West Drumoyne, and all the other 'Intermediate' schemes in Glasgow, had a Resident Factor. Rent was paid on the 28th of each month to the Factor, who had an office in his house in the scheme. He had the discretionary power to permit small arrears of rent in exceptional circumstances, and accept payments to account. In fact, it was common practice to accept weekly rather than monthly rent payments.

Early Community Life

The move to the new scheme is well remembered:

Mr G: When we flitted up here we got a covered-in van. My father said to get a covered-in van in case it was wet. And do you know how much it cost? Five shillings. That is a fact. I can always remember that. I know that because I kept hearing my parents talking about it. Because five shillings in those days was an awful lot of money. Not everybody could afford five shillings.

And:

Mr McA: It was the coalman who did it. The coalman did all the flittings. They used to say that they put blankets round their hooves when they were doing a moonlight flit!

Arriving at the new house was a memorable experience:

Mr G: It was a big improvement. It was a brand-new house that you had. We had a bath which we never had. We had an inside toilet but we never had a bath and that was important. That was a big luxury in them days if you understand what I mean.

And:

Mr McA: It seemed enormous. We had a bathroom with a bath in it which was very unusual. We also had hot and cold water, that was another thing, and a boiler in the kitchenette which was something else, but this was out of this world.

And:

Mr R: . . . to have a bathroom and to have a bath was an experience as a child that one can never forget. It was like a complete new world to belong to a house that was only one stair up. To have a kitchenette where your mother made all the food and to have a bath with hot and cold water at that age was unforgettable.

However, for some younger children of the original tenants, the move could be upsetting; this man was a boy of seven when his parents entered the brand-new scheme in 1932.

SD: Can you remember your first sight of that house?
Mr D: Yes, and it was a terrifying experience. It was awfully cold, and I

went out to play and of course it was still new and there were no fences. The back yards then had no fences and there was no front fences. I went back and I came up the wrong close and everyone had gone away and left me! I was panic-stricken. I can always remember that, going up the wrong close.

For older teenage boys already locked into the youth culture of Govan, the move was less welcome:

Mr N: Yes, I remember coming here and me and my brother hated it. We went away back to Govan. We were too far out of the road. There was nae shops and there was nothing here. There was nae school, nothing, and we didnae like it because we were away from all our pals.

As late as the 1950s and '60s, acquiring the tenancy of a house in West Drumoyne could be a memorable experience:

Mrs C: And it was marvellous to be able to get into a house that had everything, a bathroom, everything. Because I was always away in service in half-decent houses.

While most of the tenancies in West Drumoyne were allocated to overcrowded Govanites, a few were allocated through the intervention of councillors – as one might expect.

Mr R: . . . my father was in the Cleansing [Department] and he discovered that this guy that he worked with had just got engaged and had got a house in Balbeg Street and he wasn't married. So my father asked somebody why this was. I may as well mention this Councillor's name because part of the scheme was called after him. He was a local Councillor, his name was Harvie, he was employed by the Co-operative, in the Boot Department . . . My father went to see him and he asked my father what he was up for, my father explained the situation . . . He gave my father a letter for my mother to take up to Trongate the next day, and my brother got this house in Balbeg Street.

(The Trongate was the location of the Glasgow City Improvements Department, which was responsible for the letting and management of council houses.)

> SD: Was Councillor Harvie an ILP Councillor?
>
> Mr R: Yes, he was a Labour man. Now can I elaborate on this point? These houses around here were jewels in the crown.
>
> SD: When you say that, do you mean West Drumoyne or here?
>
> Mr R: In Shieldhall. [A different 'Ordinary' grade scheme to the immediate north-west of West Drumoyne, where this interview was taking place.]
>
> SD: Which was at the west side of Drumoyne?
>
> Mr R: Yes, and they called this part here Harviestown because of all his friends who stayed in this area!

(Mr R is demonstrating a well-known mechanism for obtaining accelerated access to a council house in Glasgow: support your local councillor! The ILP gained much of its political support in both tenement communities and council housing schemes precisely because of the leverage a local Councillor could exert on the housing officials. It also confirms the widespread suspicion among Glasgow council tenants that there was preferential treatment for those in the know.)

The allocation of the actual house within a given street in West Drumoyne was done randomly. This is discussed in detail in Appendix 1:

> Mr E: And when your name came up as they called it, they mentioned a street and you picked the names out of a hat.
>
> SD: Was that literally?
>
> Mr E: Yes. You picked the names out of a hat to see what house you were going to get.

With the exception of reserving the blocks of four-apartment houses in the scheme for larger families, the above observation demonstrates the lack of fine tuning in the house-allocation policy – for example, reserving ground-floor houses for the physically disabled.

An interesting anomaly in the West Drumoyne scheme was the construction of 56 four-in-a-block 'flatted houses' on a small site immediately to the

Figure 4.1 West Drumoyne shops and housing

north across Shieldhall Road. Nineteen families who had been housed since 1920 in temporary wooden Army huts type 'HB' in Crosslea Street, West Craigton, were moved en masse into these 'flatted houses'. We have already noted that these houses were probably built as a 'screen' to protect the white-collar workers and labour aristocrats in the douce Drumoyne 'Ordinary' scheme from the envious eyes of the mere manual workers in 'Intermediate' tenements. It seems reasonable to conclude that the nineteen families from the wooden huts were allocated this superior housing as a 'reward' for thirteen years in temporary accommodation.

Early Community Life

West Drumoyne's superior status, as an 'Intermediate' scheme, to 'Rehousing' schemes in the Govan area was recognised by Housing Department officials and tenants alike. This category of scheme was intended to cater for the 'general needs' of those workers excluded from 'Ordinary' schemes both by their high rent level and housing-allocation practice. Such workers were also excluded from 'Rehousing' schemes by having too high an income. These differences in status are clearly expressed by the following tenant as late as 1954, when she transferred into West Drumoyne from a local 'Rehousing' scheme known as the 'Wine Alley':

> Mrs H: I went up to West Drumoyne and the Factor says: 'I know your face.' I says, 'I know *your* face.' And he looked at me. 'Do you belong to the "Wine Alley"?' He says, 'We don't want "Wine Alley" people up here.'

What this Factor is demonstrating is the naked prejudice against people living in 'Rehousing' schemes; they were inevitably perceived by officials as 'roughs' who were not wanted in 'respectable' 'Intermediate' schemes. Mrs H had in fact been required to transfer out of the 'Wine Alley' as both she and her husband were working, and thus were above the income threshold for a 'Rehousing' scheme. Further, it transpired that the Resident Factor in West Drumoyne had quite improperly promised the tenancy to someone else. Such promises were not the prerogative of Corporation Factors but were, in fact, a not infrequent occurrence, and led to a widespread belief in Glasgow that graft and corruption were endemic in the allocation of council houses.

> Mrs H: The neighbour downstairs who was holding the keys, came up. And he says, 'Do you know Mrs MacDonald has got everything ready, he [the Factor] promised her in the Church just to get everything all ready and she thought she'd walk into that hoose.'

The West Drumoyne women's intelligence agency had in fact checked Mrs J out even before her arrival by interrogating an *earlier* migrant from the 'Wine Alley':

> Mrs H: There was a woman came up here before me [from the 'Wine Alley']. She went into a four-apartment. She used to stay in Rafford Street in the 'Wine Alley'. She got telt that a Mrs J was coming up from the 'Wine Alley', and she says, 'Well, if it's the Mrs J I know, you will have nae bother.'

The local women were involved in checking out the incomer from the 'Wine Alley' precisely because the stigma attached to this 'Rehousing' scheme was so widespread in the Greater Govan area.

The superior status of West Drumoyne as *the* 'Intermediate' scheme in the south-west of Glasgow was recognised both by its tenants and the tenants of local 'Rehousing' schemes alike. A post-Second World War incomer to West Drumoyne from Teucharhill, a small Govan 'Rehousing' scheme, said:

> Mrs B: Oh yes, it was a lovely scheme. I wouldn't come here earlier. It was for toffs, all church-going and refined. I thought my boys would be too wild and get in trouble.

This superior status is also recalled by the son of an original tenant who moved in as a child:

> Mr R: West Drumoyne was really a very happy scheme. There was no vandalism or depredation or such. I must say that it must have been one of the finest schemes in Glasgow if not Britain, because everybody looked after their garden and one was slightly better than the other. We created an environment of trying to better the surroundings and the environment . . . Our life as children was very, very good. People seemed to think that they were poverty days. As children, it was a happy life.

This atmosphere persisted into the post-war years:

> Mrs H: It was a lovely scheme. Do you know that the kids couldn't take one leaf off a tree without the neighbours about shouting at their neck.

The predominantly blue-collar shipyard-worker status of the scheme outlined at the beginning of this section demonstrates that interwar and immediate postwar council housing in Glasgow was intrinsically tied up with the structure and trajectory of the local economy. This is confirmed by the memories of original families.

> Mr E: Within the close, in the family down the stairs, the man was an engineer . . . The people across from us, he was a riveter at that time but he was unemployed and he had two boys and two girls.

And:

> Mr F: But right up and down the street they were all shipwrights, platers, riveters, tram-drivers. The people who had jobs was in the Corporation, railways, Post Office and things like that, or in the shipyards.

In the pre-war years, some of the married women worked as cleaners:

> Mr K (born 1925, talking of his mother): The only time I recollect her working she did her cleaner at night.

And:

> Mr S (born 1917, talking of his mother): . . . my mother worked for a wee while cleaning houses for better-off folk. She had one house in 'Dear Drumoyne', and some in Partick. She cleaned houses and worked for extra money.

('Dear Drumoyne' refers to the adjacent 'Ordinary' scheme of cottage houses built under the 1919 Act, with dearer rents.)
And:

> Mr McV (born 1927, talking of his mother): My mother worked, yes. She worked as a char-lady.

These observations, and the earlier observations about maids in Mosspark, remind us that in the interwar years it was still not uncommon for working-class women to be employed in domestic service, especially during the exigencies of the Depression.

The Co-operative factories, not far away on one big site at Shieldhall, were a major employer of local unmarried girls:

> Mr O'D: There were a lot of young girls worked in there. They used to leave school and there were that many factories round there. There was what you could call a jeely work. That was the jam factory. The coffee department, and – it was all young girls working in there. A lot of young girls worked in Shieldhall.

In the postwar years, this local work for West Drumoyne continued, but now included married women:

> SD: Did the women do paid work?
> Mrs O: Oh goodness yes, they had to. The men's wages were low. A lot worked in Shieldhall at the boot factory or tobacco factory. A few worked in the Southern General Hospital and, of course, in the shops.

> Mrs M: I worked in the Co-operative Dairy in Mosspark.
> Mrs C: Oh yes, most of the women worked. A lot went cleaning in the big houses in Ibrox or the Shields [Pollokshields], or doing stairs.

Yet for all its respectable-working-class status, the reality of poverty during the Depression reached into West Drumoyne. For example, people in the scheme economised with their electricity:

> Mr D: I can remember one time they called Daviot Street the street of a thousand candles. I can always remember that. You know how they [schemes] get nick-names like 'Spam Valley' and 'Wine Alley' – West Drumoyne was the 'scheme of a thousand candles'. That was because the people were canny with the electricity . . . It was like that up until after the war.

In passing, it is interesting to note that all round Glasgow, the new 'Intermediate' and 'Rehousing' schemes were frequently given nicknames. The term 'Spam Valley' was applied to housing schemes where it was alleged that the tenants, whatever their pretensions, were so poor that they subsisted on Spam sandwiches. The 'scheme of a thousand candles' was called 'Candleriggs' elsewhere and, apart from the above nicknames, 'The Jungle' was in Possil, while another, Kintra Street in Govan, was 'The Promised Land', because an unwise Councillor had promised a new house in the scheme to too many of his local voters! And as will be demonstrated, South Pollok acquired not one but three nicknames. The semantics of these nicknames suggest envy on the part of locals who were not allocated a house in these new schemes, who responded by belittling the lucky tenants. It was the housing scheme analogy of the well-known put-down of an allegedly snobbish woman: 'See her? Fur coat and nae knickers.'

In terms of religion, West Drumoyne seems to have been more successful in integrating Catholics and Protestants than Mosspark. The general perception of the tenants was that the scheme was mixed.

> Mr M: There was some went to chapel, some went to church, and some didnae bother.

And:

> SD: Was the scheme mixed religiously?
>
> Mrs D: Oh yes, but more Protestant than Catholic. But there were no problems.

Mrs J, the postwar incomer from the 'Wine Alley', and a Catholic herself, reinforced the Protestant majority thesis.

> Mrs J: Naw, it was a more Protestant scheme. Even now, in my close, I am the only Catholic. It is nearly all Protestants.

It is probable that a majority of the original tenants of West Drumoyne *were* Protestants, as the skilled manual workers of Glasgow's contemporary shipyards and engineering shops were predominantly Protestant. Nonetheless, all the tenants I interviewed were adamant that sectarianism was not a problem in the scheme.

> Mr T: It was a mixed scheme, but we, us children, never bothered about religion, because your best pal might be a Protestant, and your other pal could be a Catholic. Children never bothered about that.
>
> SD: Did the adults bother about it?
>
> Mr T: Not to my knowledge.
>
> SD: So sectarianism wasn't an issue in everyday life?
>
> Mr T: It never bothered us in Drumoyne.

Summary

All in all, then, West Drumoyne was an outstanding success in housing the kind of worker it was supposed to – blue-collar workers – in decent accommodation at 'Intermediate' rents. (It was quickly established that no family with an income in excess of £4 per week could qualify for a house in an 'Intermediate' scheme.[8]) The occupational composition remained stable until after the Second World War, with 81 per cent of the population being skilled and semi-skilled workers in 1935; 80 per cent in 1938; and 70 per cent in 1948. Workers in shipbuilding, engineering, the metal trades and transport remained the biggest occupational grouping.

West Drumoyne was a happy and self-supporting scheme, truly

'Intermediate' in terms of respectability between the gentility of Mosspark and the rumbustiousness of Blackhill, and, for the first time in Glasgow, truly meeting the 'general needs' of the local working class. It was a credit to the versatility of John Wheatley's 1924 Housing Act.

Table 4.1 West Drumoyne occupational structure, 1935–1948

% by column	1935	1938	1948
White-collar	1	1	1
Skilled manual	47	47	45
Semi-skilled manual	34	33	25
Unskilled manual	14	17	11

Notes

NB: All references preceded by 'GCA' refer to the Glasgow City Archives.

1. *Corporation Minutes*, Print No. 17, p. 1877, 6 June 1929: Sub-Committee on Sites and Buildings.
2. *Corporation Minutes*, Print No. 12, p. 1166, 5 April 1929: Sub-Committee on Sites and Buildings.
3. *Corporation Minutes,* Print No. 8, 6 December 1929: Sub-Committee on Sites and Buildings.
4. *Corporation Minutes*, Print No. 11, 21 March 1930: Sub-Committee on Sites and Buildings.
5. *Glasgow Herald*, 5 April 1930.
6. *Govan Press*, 11 April 1930, p. 8: Letters to the Editor.
7. *Govan Press*, 18 April 1930, p. 8: Letters to the Editor.
8. GCA D-HE/5/3/17: *Housing Notes:* Allocation of Housing Schemes for Particular Needs: 'Intermediate Schemes', p. 2.

5

Blackhill: Out of the Slums

Preamble

Blackhill was an exemplar – and without a doubt the best-known – of Glasgow's third category of housing scheme: 'Slum-Clearance'/'Rehousing'. (The terms were and are interchangeable locally.) It was, therefore, not only the antithesis of Mosspark in terms of its tenants, but also distinctly different from both Hamiltonhill and West Drumoyne. Hamiltonhill was a one-off small experimental 'Slum-Clearance' scheme, while the latter was an 'Intermediate' scheme housing skilled and semi-skilled manual workers. Blackhill housed labourers – the poor, put simply – and was one of a series of similar schemes including Teucherhill, Moorepark (the 'Wine Alley'), Kintra Street, Possil and Lilybank.

The Legislation

We have seen that the 1930 'Greenwood' – the Labour Minister of Health – and 1935 Housing Acts were designed to attack the mass of working-class slum tenements which remained untouched by the provisions of the 1919, 1923 and 1924 Acts. While the 1919 Housing Act was supposed to have catered for the 'general needs' of the working class, the data from Mosspark revealed that few if any manual workers were housed in the so-called 'Ordinary' schemes built under its provisions. The slums remained unaffected. Thus, throughout the 1920s there was considerable national agitation on the housing question. This culminated in the Second Labour Government's 'Crusade to End the Slums'. No less a person than the Prince of Wales involved himself in this campaign:

> I personally inspected many such places and I have been appalled that such conditions can exist in a civilised country such as ours. Every generation has a dominating social task, and so let our age, our generation, be remembered as the one in which we swept away this blot that disgraces our national life.[1]

The 1930 Housing Act was essentially aimed at demolishing slums in relatively small-scale 'clearance' or 'improvement' areas. Its subsidies were related not to the number of houses built, but to the number of slum-dwellers rehoused. The rationale was that the provisions of this Act would make it easier to deal with large, poor families housed in rotten slums. However, it soon became evident that this Act was barely touching the vast numbers of people *overcrowded* in small, sub-standard housing. Thus the 1935 Housing Act was passed, specifically targeting the problem of overcrowding in such slums.

As we have seen, in Glasgow the housing problem in the interwar years was of immense proportions.[2] After 1935 Glasgow Corporation's response to this problem was to combine the provisions of the 1930 and 1935 Housing Acts in a general large-scale slum-clearance programme. The schemes built under the provisions of these Acts were described as 'Slum-Clearance' or 'Rehousing'. They were monochromatic and visually bleak because of the Corporation's own uncoloured concrete hollow block walls, utterly devoid of architectural ornamentation, and their layout monotonous to a degree. There was no attempt at comprehensive urban planning and, initially, there were no services whatsoever in the scheme: no shops, no pub, no public library, no community centre, no GP, no churches. The minimal front 'gardens' and back-courts were a sea of mud when the first tenants moved in. It is hard to escape the conclusion that if the national housing policy had moved to the bottom end of the market, the appearance of these housing schemes accurately reflected the low esteem in which slum-dwellers were held in the interwar years.

The subsidy system available under the Acts was insufficient to acquire expensive land in the city centre, where the poor were not wanted anyway. Consequently the sites on which 'Rehousing' schemes were built were as often as not environmentally disadvantaged; this was particularly true of Blackhill. This particular scheme can, therefore, be regarded as a Glasgow exemplar of a national British housing policy designed to tackle the problem

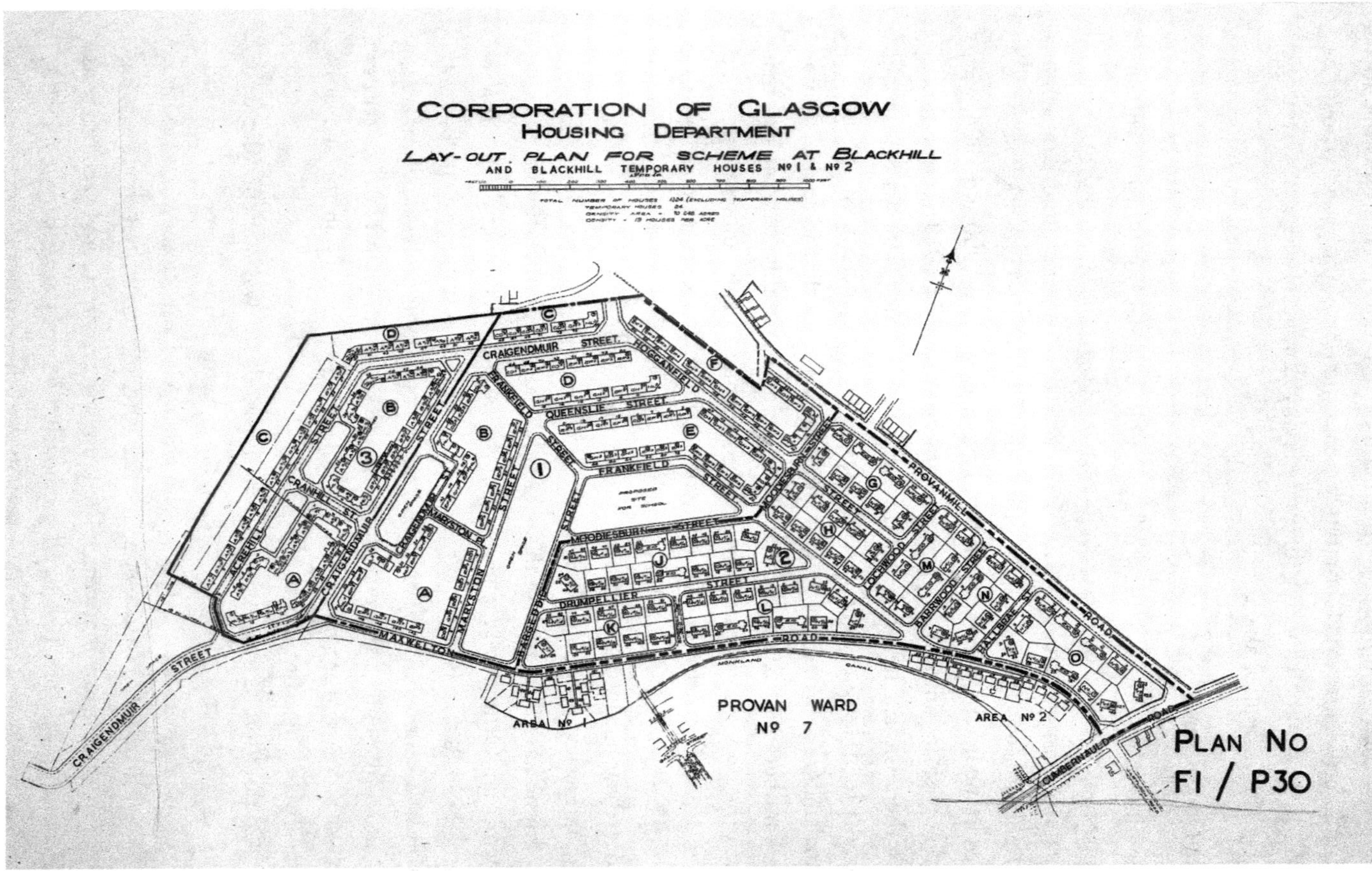

Figure 5.1 Blackhill layout

of overcrowded slum housing. It can also be regarded, ironically, as the now Labour Party-controlled Corporation's continuation of the previous policy of poor-quality council housing for 'undeserving' tenants. There was no strategic change in this policy at all.

Site Development

The hilly area known as Blackhill, a couple of miles north-east of the city centre, was acquired by the Corporation of Glasgow in 1895, and an 18-hole golf course for the Glasgow Golf Club developed on the site. Many senior Corporation officials belonged to this club. The Provan Gasworks was developed immediately to the west of the golf course between 1900 and 1904, with a railway siding into it; a large extension was added in 1919. To the north-west there was a sulphur chemical works. To the north were a distillery and a feeder road, beyond which was Glasgow's Jewish cemetery. The Monkland Canal and a series of locks bounded the site to the south, and to the east was the Cumbernauld Road. An important point about this location was that given the proximity of the gasworks and chemical plant, and the prevailing wind being from the south-west, when it blew, the site was enveloped in atmospheric pollution, including the pervasive smell of gas. It was physically and geographically marginalised, like so many similar schemes – Ferguslie Park in Paisley, for example.

Immediately to the south across the canal was the Riddrie housing scheme, an 'Ordinary' scheme built in the early 1920s under the provisions of the 1919 Act. In Glasgow terms, this meant that, just like Mosspark, it was far from 'Ordinary'; it was an élite scheme containing professionals, managers and white-collar workers, and workers in the foreman and supervisory grades. Some of these tenants were guaranteed to look upon the arrival of slum-dwellers nearby with horror.

Corporation records show that the Blackhill site was first considered for housing development in the 1920s, as an 'Intermediate' scheme, and eventually acquired in the early 1930s. The golf course was closed on 11 March 1933, with invitations to tender for the construction of 606 houses being advertised in May of that year.[3] The houses were constructed specifically as a 'Rehousing' scheme; that is, all the housing was in three-storey tenements. The first tenants moved in in April 1935, and there were 116 tenants on the

Valuation Roll a month later, with the last of the 606 houses in the first part of the scheme tenanted by January 1936. A two-apartment house cost £248 to build, and a three-apartment £276 – about 25 per cent of the cost of a house in Mosspark. The *Glasgow Herald* reported the Corporation's approval of the Blackhill plans in May 1934, and was then silent about the scheme until after the war. The Lord Provost was not present at its opening. Geographically, the scheme was totally isolated; it was on the road to nowhere.

However, it would be a mistake to view Blackhill as a homogenous housing scheme. In the pre-war years it contained at least three distinct sub-areas, while in the immediate postwar years a fourth and fifth were added. The first two sub-areas were the Blackhill 'tenements', and the third the 'four-in-a-block' houses in the higher part of the scheme, as a local describes:

> PK: Most of the people in the lower part of Blackhill were of labouring skills and no trade. The people up the road had trades and some of them were even clerical workers.
>
> SD: This is in the top part of the scheme?
>
> PK: This is in what they called 'Upper Riddrie', they preferred to call themselves as 'Upper Riddrie', some of them.
>
> SD: Rather than . . . ?
>
> PK: They didn't want to know about us, and that created prejudice because they were better dressed and it was noticeable, they were into the church in a big way. Because of that there was friction with the younger people. There were pitched battles between the young boys, regularly in the summer holidays when the schools were off, throwing bricks at each other in what was known as the Maryston Park which separated Upper Riddrie from Blackhill.
>
> SD: Between the sort of toffee-nose kids and your lot?
>
> PK: Well, supposed toffee-nosed, they weren't that toffee-nosed because they could fight back quite well.

'Upper Riddrie' did not exist officially; it was a name the tenants of this scheme invented in an effort to distance themselves socially from the slum-clearees in the adjacent 'Rehousing' scheme – a phenomenon which occurs in Glasgow to this day. The so-called 'Upper Riddrie' was in fact an 'Intermediate' scheme.

The fourth sub-area comprised the 'verandah flats' built in the postwar years, while the fifth was the small prefab development which was added on the south side of the scheme in the same period.

Tenanting Blackhill

It is safe to say that as far as Blackhill (and all other 'Rehousing' scheme) tenants were concerned, the house allocation system was totally authoritarian. Whole blocks in nearby slum neighbourhoods were designated as Clearance Areas, and the tenants were shipped out *en bloc* to Blackhill. There was no pretence at consultative or participatory procedures. As often as not, the first the tenant knew of the impending demolition of his/her house was the arrival of a Housing Department 'Nurse Inspectress'. This person would inspect the old house and tell the tenant that all verminous bedding and clothing was to be discarded. The Corporation would provide iron bedsteads in the new houses at the not insignificant extra cost of 1/- per week on the rent. The evidence makes it plain that the whole process was authoritarian and accompanied by the strictest regulation and supervision. It has been detailed for a Govan 'Rehousing' scheme elsewhere.[4] The importance the Corporation attached to the process of rehousing is encapsulated in the following quotation:

> The results of rehousing are of great sociological importance . . . the system of supervision of tenants has now evolved into a definite routine procedure. This is difficult and delicate work, the success of which depends on the sociological instincts, wide experience, and knowledge of life possessed by those selected for this duty.[5]

It is disconcerting to think that the contemporary medical profession perceived the practice of sociology to be social control, rather than critical social scientific analysis. However, that social control, or social engineering, was a national rather than simply a Clydeside phenomenon; it existed in all British towns and cities. But it was elaborated in Glasgow in a series of publications, usually emanating from the City Improvements and Public Health Departments, which spell out the implications in detail. The following excerpt is from the 1930 Annual Housing Report of Glasgow Corporation:

> I desire again to emphasise the social aspects of housing enterprise, especially as regards rehousing operations. Management involves something more than the collection of rents and attention to repairs, and implies attention to human and social needs. As a result of experience and observation over the last few years, it can be affirmed that the majority of tenants will respond to efforts made to improve their environment, but the extent of the response depends on the degree of wise and helpful aid rendered by appropriate officers of the Local Authority. In Glasgow there is for this purpose a system of close co-operation between the Public Health Department and the City Improvements Department, responsible for the management of the new schemes. The former has undertaken, through specially delegated lady inspectors, the function of routine inspection, assistance, advice and general supervision, exercised in a variety of ways for the purpose of maintaining standards of occupancy at the highest possible level.[6]

What did the 'wise and helpful aid' consist of? Here is the answer supplied by the very first of the 'lady inspectors', Miss Mathieson:

> Slum clearance houses, as regards cleanliness and order, are placed in three categories – 'clean', 'fair', and 'dirty' – the last two being regarded as unsatisfactory, and it is these groups with which I have to deal particularly.
>
> Generally speaking, 64% of the new tenants give complete satisfaction. A large proportion of the houses occupied by them are neatly and even artistically furnished . . . Houses in the 'fair' category amount to about 26% of the whole. In this group the tenants clearly show that they understand the need for cleanliness and tidiness, but unless there is constant and helpful supervision, some of them would quickly drift into a worse condition. In some cases it is difficult to draw a line of demarcation between the two categories, and I may say that the particular group into which these houses may be placed varies from time to time . . .
>
> There remains a group, which varies in the different schemes and which may be roughly computed at about 10%, who may be regarded as difficult or even incorrigible tenants.[7]

In the 1930s in Glasgow, the 'wise and helpful aid' would seem to be isomorphic with an unapologetic and relentless pressure towards domestic cleanliness which, as John Wesley pointed out, is next to godliness.

Be that as it may, the 'sociological importance' of this rehousing process is literally inscribed in the 'Draft Roll', the register of all original tenants in 'Intermediate' and 'Slum-Clearance' schemes. The richness of the data contrasts strikingly with that contained in the rental roll of the original Mosspark tenants. The only data given in the latter, apart from address and rent within the scheme, was the tenants' occupations. By contrast, the Blackhill Draft Roll contains the address of the tenants' *original* house, rent and number of rooms in that house, number, age and gender of family members, tenants' occupations, rent in the new houses, etc. It is obvious that the Corporation felt it had the right if not the duty to observe and classify their 'Rehousing' scheme tenants in such a detailed manner. It is precisely the importance of the contemporary 'sociological experiment' which permits us to provide the following detailed profile of the first tenants of Blackhill.

The biggest single group of original Blackhill tenants (N=237, or 39 per cent) came from the Garngad area of the Townhead Ward in the north-east quadrant of Glasgow's inner city. Therefore it is important to consider the characteristics of this neighbourhood briefly. By the 1930s the Garngad had an unenviable reputation in a city full of neighbourhoods with bad reputations. It even had two nicknames: 'The good and the bad' (rhyming slang) and 'Little Ireland'. The latter signifies that the population was predominantly made up of the descendants of nineteenth-century Irish Catholic migrants.

A major industrial undertaking in the Garngad – and one well-known to locals, as we shall see – was the Tharsis Copper & Sulphur Co. Ltd.[8] This famous metal-extraction plant basically produced copper from burnt iron pyrites by William Henderson's 'wet' process. The detritus from this process is universally known as 'Blue Billy', and both it and the original raw material were well-known in the Garngad. A retired Town Councillor for the area in her eighties told me that she believed this detritus caused chronic environmental pollution, which probably had something to do with the high rates of pulmonary and respiratory diseases which characterised the Garngad.[9]

During the 1930s the city of Glasgow was experiencing the worst effects of the Depression. Consequently there was a great deal of poverty and unemployment in the Garngad. Put simply, there was very little work about. This poverty was, of course, exacerbated by a lack of occupational skill. But the fact that the Garngad was a manual, unskilled, working-class area should not be allowed to obscure another fact, that familial and communal survival required an impressive battery of personal and social skills.

A final burden which locals had to bear in the interwar years was sectarian discrimination in the labour market. The many engineering works in northern and eastern Glasgow, for example the Springburn locomotive works, Braby's, and Beardmore's Forge at Parkhead, routinely did not employ Catholics, according to locals. As a consequence, the predominantly Catholic people of the Garngad were last into employment, and first out. This silent battle, which was to pursue them into Blackhill, is remembered bitterly.

There are two things which immediately strike the eye on examining the Blackhill Draft Roll: firstly, the predominance of the occupation of 'labourer' and, secondly, the predominance of Irish names among the tenants. Of the 605 original tenants (the 606th tenant was the Resident Factor):

- 261 were 'labourers';
- 64 were 'widows', 'spinsters' and single women involved in 'domestic duties';
- 28 were 'carters';
- 12 were 'steelworkers';
- 12 were 'miners'.

There are difficulties in stating what constituted a 'labourer' decades after the event. Suffice it to say that this category covered a wide range of incomes from the lowest to the highest in the scheme. The second category – widows, spinsters and domestic duties – is very interesting. It is plain from an analysis of the data in the Draft Roll that a large number of single women entered as having 'domestic duties' had children. They were, in other words, single-parent families. In any event, this category of women tenants is significantly bigger than that in the Govan 'Rehousing' scheme I have also studied intensively.[10]

On the point about Irish surnames, their presence in large numbers does imply the presence of a substantial number of Catholics in Blackhill. We have already demonstrated their near-total absence from Mosspark. Indeed, the diversity of the slum population whence the first Blackhill tenants came is evidenced by the fact that, apart from Scottish and Irish surnames, at least one each from the following ethnic groups can be identified in the Draft Roll: Italian, French, Lithuanian, British Honduras, Indian and Russian Jewish.

Apart from the Garngad, original tenant families came from the following Wards of Glasgow, the largest number first:

Townhead:	97
Calton:	76
Anderston:	20
Cowcaddens:	13
Mile-end:	12

Remembering that the Garngad is in Townhead Ward, we can readily see that the vast majority of the first tenants of Blackhill came from a well-defined area in the north-east inner city. (If one added the Garngad and Townhead families together, they would form 57 per cent of original tenancies.) Thus, dense pre-existing social networks of kin and neighbours were transferred *en bloc* to the new housing scheme. While this was very important for the continuation of community and communality, I do not think Corporation officials expected this, because of their firm conviction that slum-dwellers lived in disorganised chaos.

The conditions out of which these tenants came are indicated by the presence in the Draft Roll of 31 official TB cases, 18 cases of overcrowding and 1 stark 'fire-tragedy case'. The mean wage was £2 per week, but the incomes ranged from 15/- (blind pensioner) and 17/- (domestic duties – 1 child), at the lower end of the scale, to £6.11.7d. (labourer – 7 children), £5.11.0d. (labourer – 2 children) and £4.16.0d. (carpenter – 4 children), at the highest. The largest families (there were three) contained 11 persons, of which 9 were children. But the original families were still in the child-bearing years and, subsequently, there were many larger families, including at least one with 18 persons.

The final point about the characteristics of the first tenants is that most of the incomes discussed above were fictional. Quite simply, the vast majority of these tenants were not working. A preliminary analysis of Public Assistance applications for the district containing Blackhill has turned up 26 applications for the first two months of 1936 alone. This suggests a staggering level of poverty in the scheme.

Early Community Life in Blackhill (1935–c. 1950)

The simplest thing to say about early community life in Blackhill is that there was a lot of it. Every single tenant of the many interviewed described enthusiastically a bustling, energetic, noisy and public culture, which was the complete antithesis of the staid culture of Mosspark. Furthermore, remembering that these interviews were conducted in 1990, there was unanimity that this culture lasted integrally for *at least* the first two decades of the life of the scheme, and aspects of it survived up until the 1980s. Notions of 'embourgeoisement', 'the end of the ideology', 'affluent workers' and 'you've never had it so good' would have been greeted with derision and incomprehension in Blackhill. The sheer density of this community life gives the lie to the dominant media images of Blackhill as an atomised and dysfunctional scheme.

*Flitting**

The actual move from the old tenemental house to the new house in Blackhill is well remembered; after all, it was the single most important event in many families' lives to date.

> SD: Do you actually remember the move?
>
> DF: Oh yes, I had to get a couple of pals to do the flitting. In those days it was a common thing to go down to the fishmarket to get fish for the shops. You used to hire the likes of myself and they would give you a tanner for running a wheelbarrow and taking their fish from the fishmarket to their shop. Well we hired one of them to take our belongings up here, we did it in three or four runs.

* Flitting is a Scots word meaning the process of moving house.

Setting

The beauty of the scheme's setting was also frequently remarked, which, given the environmental disadvantage mentioned above, is a telling indicator of the grim nature of the slums they had just left.

> LM: It was an adventure playground. We used to chase the rats and you got all sorts of wild life. We used to go and watch the sandpipers and the

> housemartins flying round about, the swans bred continuously. Some guys would throw things, but we used to protect them, it was a great life. We used to fish for tadpoles, baggie minnows, and there was a big coal barge which was half submerged and we used to kid on we were pirates on that. There was hot water swimming – we used to play on the locks in spite of a 40 foot drop if we fell. We used to dare each other to walk across the locks.

(The water was hot as a result of the cooling process in the adjacent chemical works, which discharged into the canal. Outsiders of course had no knowledge of these local dangers.)

Sleeping Arrangements

Although the new houses were bigger than the old, a combination of family size and poverty frequently resulted in bed-sharing. In other words, the new council houses were bigger but still not big enough, given the big, sometimes huge, families living in the slums.

> PK: We had a large family but a few of them were married by the time we moved to Blackhill. There was still about eight of us and we had a three-room-and-kitchen with a long lobby which is now called a hall. There was a small room, a middle room and a big room and then we had the living room which was the kitchen and the scullery which is now the kitchenette and a bathroom. My father and mother slept in the big room, myself, my sister Mary and my brother slept in the one bed. Myself and my brother slept at the top and my sister slept at the other end. In the middle room there was a pull-down settee that Janet slept in and Frances. Mike, when he was home – Mike was in the Merchant Navy from when he was very young – he would be sleeping in there with Pat and that was all that was left in the house, officially, seven plus my father and mother – nine. The rest was married or away somewhere.

Furniture

The tenants didn't have a lot of furniture:

> AM: What sort of furniture did you have at that time?
> MO'D: We hadn't a lot. We had a sofa and a kitchen-table which you

scrubbed and a couple of wooden arm-chairs. The authorities suggested that you didn't take your bed with you and they sold you this bed along with the house. It was like a hospital bed with a flock mattress on it, and they sold you this with a wee chest of drawers and a square of linoleum that sat in the middle of your floor, I don't know how much it was but you paid it back at a shilling a week.

But the houses were very much appreciated:

SD: Tell me what it was like when you moved in?

AD: There were two set-in beds. We moved from 34 Bright Street and we thought it was a better house. We left a room-and-kitchen and we went – there were only four of us – to a better house which had a white sink, it was all done up like a renovation. Because there was a white sink in it, that was a God-send. So we flitted over there and that was when we changed with the old guy to come over to Blackhill.

SD: So what was the house like when you moved to Blackhill? Can you remember the house?

AD: Oh it was brand new, we were the first tenants.

SD: What was it like, how many rooms did it have?

AD: It had two rooms, a toilet, and a thing we didn't have down the road – a bathroom! The toilet in the Garngad was in the close.

There were often large numbers of people in the close, the common entrance stair, in the new housing scheme.

MM: There must have been about 60 people in our stair. In the Mullans, there was Mr & Mrs Mullan – Mr Mullan worked in the steelworks at Govan – there was Willie, Andrew, Anne, Patricia, five children in there and the two adults. Down below us was McRae – Mr and Mrs McRae, Dolly, Kenneth, Donald, Mairi, Sandy and Ella – eight. The Grahams, Mr and Mrs Graham, George, Peter, Tony, Duncan, Kate, Agnes.

SD: So you're talking about 50–60 people?

MM: Oh easy, the Williams were a big family and the Mullans were a big family.

Meals

Breakfasts were informal:

> DT: We always had our porridge in the morning. My mother made sure of that. We had our tea and toast and our porridge before we went to school.
> SD: Did you actually sit down at the table and have it, all of you together?
> DT: Sometimes, but mostly we got it in bed before we got up for school.

On the Parish

Many families were 'on the Parish' (receiving Public Assistance) and were supplied with clothes for the children.

> PK: The only suits I ever remember until I got one from the Army was the Parish suits I got and they were all stamped on the inside 'Property of Glasgow Corporation', and we used to get marched down from Blackhill – we never went on buses or trams then, we called them the caurs – we never went in a caur, we walked all the way down the Budgeon, down the Royston Road, down High Street and along George Street to John Street in those days, and we were fitted for our – and it was the best of gear – herring-bone stuff, but you had to shave the inside of the vests and the pants, honestly. My brothers used to shave them and my father.
> SD: Why?
> PK: Because if you put them on in the winter they just scadded [scratched] you – they were so rough. And that was my clothing, and I was so proud of it but I must have stood out like a sore thumb! But I loved it – it was the best of gear!

Improvisation

A great deal of imaginative improvisation of clothing and furnishing went on among the women.

> MG: Down at Riddrie there was a disinfectant place and you could go and buy bleach bottles for threepence and get a great big bit of black soap on a muslin cloth. And they used to dollop it for ninepence – that's what you got your bath with.

AM: Derback soap?

MG: No, it was just black soap.

AM: Soft, was it?

MG: Soft it was, black soft soap that my mother used to lift with a ladle onto the muslin cloth. That was melted down to do the washing and put into sweetie jars. In fact, the man used to keep us flour bags and they were put in the big sink for boiling – she would get four for about half-a-crown or a shilling and put them into the boiler and boil them until all the stiffness was out them. Sometimes they had the name of the flour bags on them and she used to wring them out on the old wringer – two rollers with a handle on it, it wasn't even a wringer – and they were wrung into big sinks and that was put in with the bleach and let them lie until the name came off it and that was our sheets and pillows and curtains.

She used to go down to a place in Castle Street for throwouts – the ends of the bread or misshaped rolls or bashed cakes. It was Templeton's at Parliamentary Road then and the man used to keep her the muslin off the cheeses and that was all brought home and that was boiled, bleached and dyed. You put it in the big enamel bath tub and dyed all the curtains as well.

Jam jars and sauce bottles were all kept and gathered up till maybe it came to a half a crown and you would get money on them. You got a farthing for a jeely [jam] jar at the local shops.

My informants told me that the following 'small businesses' were run, on and off, from houses in the scheme: tobacconist, tailor, barber and grocer. Local tenants were obliged to run these businesses for themselves, as the Corporation had provided no amenities whatsoever in the scheme. There were also numerous (illegal) bookies' runners on the streets.

Women's Work

The women, in fact, worked very hard, both inside and outside of the scheme, and their daughters learned their trade as both domestic and productive labourers from an early age:

SD: When the soup was getting made, for example, did your sisters take part in that kind of work or was it usually your mother?

PK: Your mother usually done it but she brought them in. There was a sort of apprenticeship going on I think, looking back. They were encouraged to get involved with making the dinners, encouraged to help to do the ironing, she gave them wee simple tasks. She was doing her community education worker, she would give them wee tasks to do to build their confidence up, learning to sew things.

SD: So it wasn't community education, it was actually women's education, wasn't it?

PK: Community education and social work have always been there, now it's professionalised and people think it's great – the working class have always looked after themselves.

SD: It sounds like you're saying that working-class women looked after working-class men?

PK: Yes, I'd accept that, that's true – well, there were roles that were carried out.

And:

SD: Tell me a bit about hawking, like what your mother did.

PT: That was the auld basket with dishes and she walked round the doors for rags and woollens. She did outside of Glasgow, everywhere. It is still going on on a smaller scale in the present day. You took buses out to these schemes like miners' rows and that, Queenzieburn, Twechar, and all these places. It was partly worn clothing and you sold them at the Barras – it still goes on at the Briggait, Paddy's Market.

SD: Was hawking regarded as being in any way an inferior job?

PT: Oh no, the hawker was recognised as a person. It didn't come under the likes of tinkers, no way. If you were a hawker you were well off, you always got a good name, you helped people because they were earning every day and the people had nothing.

The Local Economy

In Blackhill, an alternative, highly localised but highly organised 'black' economy – a sub-culture – flourished in the scheme. This ranged from a simple exchange of neighbourly services to the organisation of 'sheets' – collections to assist in the costs of a funeral or a wake; the resale of pawn tickets; the running of 'menages'; resetting; and money-lending, the latter a complex phenomenon involving at least four stages on a continuum.

Menages

Menages – pronounced 'menodge' – were as common in Blackhill as in Hamiltonhill:

> SD: I hear a lot of talk from the women about menages and things like that. How did that work?
>
> Mrs T: Well you got a turn, you picked a number, it could be a low number and it could be the first turn or the twenty-first turn or the fifty-first turn, depending on how many were in it. If you got the first turn that was good, you got your money right away, but you still paid it every week. Some wanted it the first turn and some wanted it the last because they wanted it a few months hence. It was like money in the bank to them, they couldn't save it, a couple of shillings a week, you didn't miss it.
>
> SD: Was that a common thing in Blackhill?
>
> Mrs T: Och aye, it went on all over the place, all over Glasgow. A menage they called it. They called it the Tiddly as well, but a menage was the right name for it.
>
> SD: In this system of the menage when all the women were paying in weekly, did anybody ever cheat on it?
>
> Mrs T: Not that I know of but I dare say that it was maybe bumped at times. I never knew of any locals to bump it because they wouldn't have got away with it in those days. The women would have did them in theirselves, never mind the men.
>
> SD: Right. So it is an elementary form of working-class savings bank?
>
> Mrs T: Yes, similar to the ones they have now in the Credit Unions – not unlike a Credit Union in infancy. Looking back, it shows you the honesty of the people because once you've got your money you could say 'Stuff it', and anybody could have done that. And yet this honesty was there that people paid their money regularly even although they had their £10.
>
> SD: Did you ever hear of anybody ratting on this?
>
> Mrs T: Never to my knowledge.

It was as if Blackhill tenants recognised that people in other neighbourhoods were legitimate targets for theft, but you didn't steal from each other.

The importance and ubiquity of the menage as a cultural survival mechanism among poor working-class women in Glasgow is evidenced by a fictional but detailed discussion of one in Edward Gaitens' contemporary novel *The Dance of the Apprentices.*[11]

Money-lending

Money-lending was a commonplace among the Glasgow working class, and has always been associated with criminal violence in the popular eye. However, it is better viewed as a continuum running from interest-free loans from, usually, a local woman to neighbours and kin; to similar small loans for a little interest; to 'free-lance' money-lending for high rates of interest by a crook (in Glaswegian, a 'Ned') who would personally use violence to get this money back; to organised 'professional' money-lending by a criminal who employs a 'stick-man', or enforcer, or leg-breaker. The first two types are discussed here by Blackhill locals:

> PK: She [my mother] did everything for people in Blackhill, including non-charge money-lending. The only reason we could do that as a family was that we were all thieves, quite honestly. I was in St John's Approved School when I was thirteen. All my brothers done time.

When pressed about his mother not charging interest, this local man said:

> Well I don't know how you could convince people of that. I think that people who don't believe you, would not believe regardless of the evidence . . . I remember specifically she never took money from people, but it was only people that she knew that she gave money to and they always knew where to come. I don't know how I could prove it to anybody, I don't even need to prove it, I know it is true.

Resetting

Resetting is more commonly known as 'fencing', or the buying and selling of stolen property.

SD: Were there any other kinds of things that your mother was into in Blackhill Street?

PK: She was into resetting. Because we had money from the very sources that I have told you about – they weren't declared. If somebody does a job, for example, Micky O'Dowd at 2 o'clock in the morning batters the door – 'Who is it?', 'It's Micky'. 'Aye, okay Micky.' Micky comes in with a big roll of this thick linoleum-like stuff, our whole house was done in this stuff. Micky brought this stuff over at 2 o'clock in the morning off a couple of trucks that passed on the railway. They used to jump the trucks, bust the door, throw the stuff off that they could, damaged some but there was some that they didn't damage. The trains were going very slow, through the junction and Micky sold it to us because we had the money, and we would get it very cheaply.

Wise Women

It will be patently obvious by now that in Blackhill women were vital to the social production and reproduction of 'community'. Several were permanently 'on call'.

PK: My mother came from Ayrshire, a very, very hard-working woman. Tremendous intelligence but no skills. When I say no skills – no skills that she could work with but was respected in the community, she was the one who helped people through a birth, was sent for – in those days when a child was not well they gave them a mustard bath – she was the sort of local witch doctor. She was unbelievable. Her organisational sense was unbelievable for somebody that was supposed to be semi-literate.

PK's use of the phrase 'supposed to be' is instructive. It suggests that he is very well aware of the negative perceptions of his mother's skills which outsiders would share, which were not only offensive but also irrelevant to the harsh realities of life within the scheme.

Thieving

In Blackhill, 'nicking' was normal. The scheme contained a distinct and normalised criminal sub-culture. For what it is worth, a City Police Inspector said at a public meeting in 1950 that there were 1,000 'known criminals' in

Blackhill. (That means there would have to have been nearly two per house!) The geography of Blackhill actually lent itself to banditry:

> PK: I started stealing char. I must have been about ten. At the Provan Gasworks adjacent to Acrehill Steet at the foot of the scheme and these houses must have been built later than ours because they were of a different type of brick, different structure. We used to chap the doors and say, 'Missis, do you need char?' – this was at night – 'Aye, how many bags can you get me?' 'How many do you want? One, two, three?' You had an order for the material before you stole it. You went across to the Provanmill Gasworks, which meant crossing a busy railway line and a big stream – in fact I think the stream was the Molendinar – we would go over and steal the char and come back and sell it. That was the start of it.
>
> SD: What is char, precisely?
>
> PK: Char is what people now call coke. Coke is the product of the coal when the gas has been taken out of it.

Passing road traffic was also raided:

> PK: Another thing we did is on the Riddrie side of Blackhill at the Edinburgh Road, we're down at Alexandra Park and the Cumbernauld Road/Edinburgh Road junction – a set of lights used to be there. There's three hills – we called them the three hills – before you get to the top, going out to Millerston – what we did there during the war when the lights were out, the motors would stop there, the old motors with the old tarpaulin sheets strapped down, we would jump on the back of these tarpaulin sheets. We had prearranged at the top of the third hill at the canal bridge next to what was the tea-room which took you on to the canal bank, and you could walk all the way down in the dark. We had people sitting up on that bridge out of sight and they would watch for trucks coming up and we would jump on with a knife, crack open the tarpaulin sheet while it was going, while it was going up the hill slowly, and whatever was in there – whether it be sugar, radios, tea-cans – we would start to throw them halfway up the hill to our punters and run down the canal with them, and then we would get a torch and look to see what we had and then we would try and flog it. We couldn't get a market prior because we didn't know what we were going to get.

As was rail-traffic:

> CM: A lot of degradation* was done with the goods wagons. On the railway, stealing out the railway.
>
> SD: How did that work?
>
> CM: Well, you waited until the train slowed down and jumped on it, opened the carriage door and whatever was in it, you took it. It could be sweeties, it could be old rag bags or anything, but you took it away. Suit material and whisky were in it, they could usually tell which one had the whisky and which one had the clothes in it.

* This is a malapropism for 'depredation'.

Gangs

Blackhill is in Glasgow; Blackhill had gangs. Therefore there were gang fights, and people got hurt.

> CM: Nearly all the boys ran about in a gang, they all came into different streets and ran about the Sousies chip-shop.
>
> SD: And what was your team called?
>
> CM: We were the Easy Gang.
>
> SD: What was it all about?
>
> CM: I think it was just more than devilment or anything. You thought you were better than some of the guys that came from another scheme.
>
> SD: Did anybody ever get hurt or injured in any of these fights?
>
> CM: A lot of people injured, yes, and seriously assaulted.

The speaker himself was injured in gang fights, frequently, and jailed:

> CM: They took us to the Royal and stitched our heads up and they didn't give a damn how they stitched it and it was sore. I was more sick with that than I was with prison.

One of my informants witnessed a fatal attack on his father when he was about ten.

PK: Now Mrs Jack lived down the stair who was my father's auntie and the gang came looking for this boy Jack who was in a gang called The Easy, and my father had a drink in him and he ran down the stair to chase them – they were only young men of 17, 18 – they were too young to go in the Army and most of them left, but one came through the back and my father fell over the wall because he had drink in him and the boy stuck a bayonet through him, right through his lungs. Now he eventually died from that so it wasn't seen as murder, it was seen as manslaughter because of the timescale between the occurrence and the death and that is the way he died.

Self-entertainment

While there can be no denying that Blackhill was a tough place, street-entertainment rather than street-fighting was the norm. The single biggest participatory self-entertainment in Blackhill was football. Just as in Hamiltonhill, it would probably be safe to say that football *raged* in Blackhill every day!

> It was nearly all football, there was practically a street team in every street here and we used to all challenge one another on different Sundays. We played on a Sunday say Queenslie Street, Hogganfield Street, Frankfield Street, Drumellier Street, Craigendmuir Street.

Buskers were common:

> And the people used to come round singing – the buskers, that was a common thing in those days – on a Sunday and when you were at the top end of Maryston Street, it was 'The Old Rugged Cross' – they were giving it laldy – you could hear it everywhere. But in respect to the fact that it was mainly Protestant, they were giving it 'The Old Rugged Cross', and when they came down to Blackhill Street it was 'Hail Queen of Heaven' [a well-known Catholic hymn].[12] And because we were bandits and agile, the palings had been cut away – this was during the war – and the tops were taken away so that would be about three feet high with no tops. The mothers would wrap the money up in a paper, throw it over the window, it would land on this side of the paling, the bloke was on the other side, so we would

nip over quick, vault over the palings, get the money, and out the back – the poor bloke singing for nothing – sad but that was just what happened.

There were also 'clabbers'.

Mrs C: A 'clabber' was a get-together in the back-court. You'd put up a washing line and hing old blankets over it, sort of like a stage. We all brought our chairs out. Some would hing oot the windae, and everybody would give us a song or a dance, or something. Sometimes there would be a squeeze-box or banjo or a penny whistle, or a moothie [mouth-organ.] It was great.

Women initiated clabbers for their own fun and self-entertainment, as local men went to the Provanmill Inn, the local pub.

Card-schools were common:

PK: Card-schools were regular up the stair. In every close there would be card-schools played. Nearly every night of the week.

SD: Were they held in a house?

PK: No, out in the landing, four or five of us would sit on the landing, playing pontoon, or solo, but pontoon was the thing for the money. So there was a lot of gambling going on.

Drinking

And, of course, Blackhill was a hard-drinking scheme. Sometimes the drinking parties could assume surreal proportions, as no less an authority than sculptor and former gangster Jimmy Boyle testifies.[13]

> Blackhill is a crazy place. It was now almost three in the morning and we went into the street where some guys were sitting around a bonfire singing Celtic songs and drinking wine almost in the middle of the street . . . We sat around drinking and it was as though it was the middle of the day rather than the middle of the night.

But all early tenants were unanimous in their view that Blackhill was a friendly place in which to live.

SD: So you're painting a picture of a pretty happy, neighbourly place?

CM: I think so because we are all reared together and all our mothers and fathers were all reared together then they came up. They never split one street, they tried to get as many people as possible from the one street into the one street when they were opening up. I thought the scheme was a marvellous place.

The beauty of many gardens is vividly remembered:

SD: What were the back-courts and the gardens like at that time?
FM: Brilliant! Well-kept in every close, not everybody had an interest in their gardens but they were kept tidy, but the ones who took an interest in them, there were some lovely ones.

Factors and Green Ladies

In the first decade or so of its existence, Blackhill was heavily policed by two key officials of the Corporation: the Resident Factors and the 'Green Lady'. (The latter actually comprised three different officials, all with green uniforms: the Health Visitor from the Public Health Department, the Public Health Nurse from the same Department, and the Nurse Inspectress from the Housing Department. That locals should confuse them is not surprising; their jobs differed only in emphasis. As we have seen, their overall function was one of social control.) This policing is also well-remembered.

EH: There was two or three times when I had occasion to go into the Factor who was a Mr McKay at that time and he was a very strict disciplinarian, not only for looking after the area and making sure it was kept in order, but also rent-wise as well, as many a time I had to go round and say, 'Could you please excuse my mother and father, but they'll try and make it up the following month.' That happened two or three times with us.
SD: Did you pay your rent monthly then?
EH: Yes.
SD: And what would the Factor say to you?
EH: He never actually knocked me back but he used to be very abrupt and say, 'Well tell them they better make sure that they get it or else they will be out!' Something like that anyway.
SD: Did you used to be scared of going?

EH: Not so much scared, I didn't like the embarrassment, you had to virtually plead.

SD: How come your mother or your father didn't go, and they sent you?

EH: I think they just didn't want to face up to him – as simple as that.

I think it would be fair to say that EH's parents were ashamed to go and ask a favour of the factor.

If anything, the 'Green Lady', the 'Panshine Lady' as she was known locally, is even better remembered than the Resident Factors:

SD: Did they ever come inspecting the house?

CM: Yes, the Panshine Lady, as we used to call her. Get the dust and get they walls done and that.

SD: Who was she?

CM: A health lady. They called her Panshine, 'Get that pan tidied up.'

SD: And what kind of thing did she used to do?

CM: She would look for stoor [dust] and that, your walls and your cooker for your back-to-back grate, get it polished and get the stairs done. That was the worst thing that ever happened was taking her away. She kept them all on their toes.

SD: Were people frightened of her?

CM: No, but I think they respected her because they thought they'd better get it tidied for her coming because she would just come back until it was done.

EH is saying the same thing as Hamiltonhill tenants did. While the rigid authoritarianism of these officials was often resented, tenants perceived it as keeping their scheme 'respectable'. To this extent, it could be said that they had internalised the dominant management ideology.

Blackhill's Reputation

Whatever the complex realities of life within the scheme, by the 1950s it had a city-wide reputation which could only be described as pernicious. It was without a doubt the most stigmatised housing scheme I had ever encountered, and I have considerable personal knowledge of such places. By the end of the decade, it was – and remained until demolition in 1983 to make way for the M8 motorway – systematically black-listed for credit by local high-street chain-stores, locals found it difficult to get work if a Blackhill address was given, and city taxi-drivers were loath to pick up fares within the scheme. Blackhill subsequently became the topic of numerous *national* media programmes, including a particularly insensitive 1975 Thames Television documentary in which the investigator was Jonathan Dimbleby.

Blackhill tenants knew about this stigma and bitterly resented it. They actually have their own explanations for it. These include the geographical isolation of the scheme; the presence of the adjective 'Black' in its title; the fact that prisoners escaping from nearby Barlinnie jail would always be hid in the scheme, in false cupboards built for the purpose; and an alleged postwar Glasgow Corporation policy of 'dumping riff-raff' there.

My belief is that a combination of two factors, one general and one specific, combined to give Blackhill its evil reputation. The first factor is the general criminality of the area. There can be no doubt that many of the (male) residents of the scheme had criminal records. This is not the place to rehearse well-known arguments about 'criminal areas', and their meaning. But it must be acknowledged that the raiding of railway wagons and passing lorries was systematically perpetrated by some scheme residents in the first twenty years or so of its life. (We turn to the reasons for this below.) And Blackhill *was* a place in which stolen property could easily be disappeared, and where it was very difficult for the police to obtain intelligence. Further, local men were both victims and perpetrators of murders, as well as being involved in the ubiquitous gang-fights. And the presence of a handful of professional criminal families involved in internecine vendettas ensured that Blackhill's reputation for violent crime flourished in a city which thrives on such stories. The Glasgow 'hard men' die hard, both literally and metaphorically. We should not be surprised if Glaswegians themselves assist in the reproduction of such legends, for stigmata have real effects. The effects are amplified by such books as Alexander McArthur's *No Mean City*, James Patrick's *A Glasgow Gang Observed* and Jimmy Boyle's *A Sense of Freedom*.[14]

Poisoning

This background, important as it may be, pales into insignificance compared with the second specific incident which in my judgement drove the final nail into Blackhill's reputational coffin. This was the death of nine scheme residents due to poisoning by illegal 'hooch' early in 1949. This terrible incident left such a mark on the collective consciousness of Glaswegians in general – not to mention Blackhill residents – that I have no doubt whatsoever that this was the single biggest factor in the reproduction of the Blackhill stigma. I should say that at the time of the original research – 1989/90 – and to this day, kin of the victims were still alive. Some of these people did not wish to talk about this incident and indeed refused to discuss it with me. However, as will be evident, others did, in an exceptionally sensitive way.

Basically, the incident occurred at the Hogmanay/New Year celebrations at the end of 1948/beginning of 1949. Locals tell the story:

> FG: A young man who went about with him, Freddy Maloney, had got a job in a chemical works down at the two bridges along Royston Road and there was this big tank of alcohol, and to him alcohol was whisky and he is at a party on Hogmanay and they were all drinking and the drink was finished. So he says, 'If you get some empty bottles, I can take you to where you can fill them.' And he took them into the works and they filled their own bottles – and there was ten people died.
>
> AM: What happened about that?
>
> FG: It was poison – it was methyl alcohol. It is used in paints and aircrafts, it was industrial alcohol. He lived for a week. I wasn't at the party, I was working in the hospital and when I came home I never saw him until the next day and when he came in he looked ill and I asked him what had happened to him and he says, 'Oh I don't know, I'll go out and get some fresh air.' He went away out until night time and his sister came down and says, 'Dick's been up my ma's all day.' I said that he had left to go to the Inn and she said, 'He went to the Inn and someone took him down the road because he felt so ill.' He had something to eat and it helped him a wee bit and he was able to live for the week but the alcohol had went through his system, the doctors told me he would have been a vegetable if he had lived. It had washed the fat from the back of his eyes, he was blind. I knew what he was trying to say to me but no-one else did. I prayed for him to die, I didn't want to watch him suffer.

At the time of this tragedy, there were four daily papers and three evening papers appearing in Glasgow, not to mention weeklies, Sunday papers and popular magazines. Every single one of the daily and evening papers, and many of the weekly/Sunday papers, covered this story with banner headlines on page 1. Examples include:

THREE DEATHS AFTER PARTY
Seven others Taken to Hospital
Glasgow Tragedy
Glasgow Herald, 4 January 1949

EIGHT DEATHS AFTER PARTY –
ALCOHOL POISON TRAGEDY
Glasgow Herald, 5 January 1949

POLICE TRACE SOURCE OF POISON LIQUOR
CID Question Chemical Works Employee
Glasgow Eastern Standard, 10 January 1949

GLASGOW POISONING: 3 DEAD
CID IN 3 a.m. Drink Probe
Daily Record, 4 January 1949

6 DEAD AFTER PARTY IN GLASGOW HOUSE
13 ARE DETAINED IN HOSPITAL;
POISONING CAUSE OF TRAGEDY?
Evening Times, 4 January 1949

It *was* methyl alcohol stolen from the chemical works, and in some cases diluted with lemonade or cheap wine, which caused this tragedy. But it is instructive that the Blackhill man quoted above said that locals felt it was unfair that the man who stole the industrial alcohol should have been imprisoned for it. It was almost as if Blackhill was the kind of housing scheme where such a disaster was to be expected, and tenants knew it.

Summary

In its first few decades of existence, Blackhill was an impoverished, largely unskilled, manual working-class community characterised by a variety of familial and social survival strategies, including elaborate collective self-help mechanisms largely organised by women, and thieving, largely organised by men. Most heads of households were characterised as unskilled, most described as 'labourers'. It was a tough place, where one had to be tough to survive. But the real violence was that of poverty, which Blackhill tenants combated with humour, imagination and resilience. One long-term woman resident said:

> I just love Blackhill. I'll not let anyone say anything against it because if you were in trouble or you needed anything, you could always go and chap on a door, but you can't do that now.

And, as a long-serving local Councillor put it to me:

> Blackhill had a pawky humour, and a great appreciation of humour. Locals were clever people, well able to evaluate arguments.

Their humour is seen in their nicknaming of the 'Green Ladies' as 'Buggy Annie' and 'Panshine'. They too had a moral order in their community, but most likely incomprehensible to the douce residents of Mosspark.

For reasons which remain unclear, the occupational structure of Blackhill underwent significant change just before the Second World War. The proportion of skilled manual workers nearly quadrupled, while the unskilled fell by two-thirds. The best hypothesis is that unskilled workers who could not afford the rent voted with their feet and left the scheme, while the advent of war meant fuller local employment for skilled workers.

Table 5.1 Blackhill occupational structure, 1936–1938

% by column	1936	1938
Skilled manual	10	38
Semi-skilled manual	5	15
Unskilled	74	24
Women	11	6

Notes

NB: All references preceded by 'GCA' refer to the Glasgow City Archives.

1. Quoted in Branson, N. and M. Heineman (1973), *Britain in the 1930s*, Panther, p. 210.
2. Damer (1989), op. cit.: pp. 60ff.
3. *Corporation Minutes*, Print No.7, p. 726, 1934–35: Housing Committee.
4. Damer (1989), op. cit.
5. *Annual Report of the Medical Officer of Health for Glasgow*, 1929.
6. GCA D-HE/1/5/35-37, p. 7.
7. GCA D-HE/6/7/139: Scottish National Housing & Town Planning Committee Edinburgh Conference, 19/20 April 1928: Miss C. Mathieson, Public Health Department, Glasgow: *Supervision of Tenants in Slum Clearance Schemes*, pp. 2–3.
8. Checkland, S. (1967), *The Mines of Tharsis: Roman, French and British Enterprise in Spain*, Allen & Unwin.
9. Personal communication, former Councillor the late Mrs Agnes Ballantyne (real name). Checkland does not appear to have investigated the health consequences of the Tharsis plant in his study.
10. Damer (1989), op. cit.
11. Gaitens, E. (1948), *The Dance of the Apprentices*, Canongate Classics 31, Book 2, Chapter 1, pp. 139–48.
12. This ability of back-court buskers to identify Catholic and Protestant sub-neighbourhoods in tenemental areas is also described fictionally by Gaitens, pp. 63–4.
13. Boyle, J. (1977), *A Sense of Freedom*, Pan, p. 84.
14. McArthur, A. and H. Kingsley Long, (1935), *No Mean City*, Longmans, Green; Patrick, J. (1973), *A Glasgow Gang Observed*, Neil Wilson Publishing; and Boyle (1977), op. cit.

6

Craigbank: Amateur Dramatics?

Legislation

Craigbank, an 'Ordinary' scheme constructed under the 1946 Housing Act, is one of the constituent schemes within the Pollok housing estate. This land, south-west of the city centre, constituted the ancestral estate of Sir John Stirling Maxwell; Glasgow Corporation entered into negotiations with him as early as 1934 with a view to purchasing it. Maxwell was interested in town planning and did not want the Corporation to build monotonous housing schemes, but in actual fact the local authority resented his interference.[1]

Pollok is one of Glasgow's four large postwar peripheral housing schemes, the other three being Castlemilk, Drumchapel and Easterhouse – 'deserts wi' windaes', in Billy Connolly's immortal phrase. But outsiders perennially view Pollok as a homogenous housing scheme. This is simply not the case. An excellent, forensic but unfortunately unpublished analysis of the historic development of the Pollok schemes has been provided by Mooney.[2] Suffice it to say here that, as distinct from the other three peripherals, Pollok contained substantial pre-war as well as postwar council housing developments. Insofar as outsiders know anything about Pollok, this is the only characteristic of which they are aware. Briefly, greater Pollok can be considered to contain the following distinct sub-areas: Old Pollok, Old Nitshill and Househillwood (pre-war); and West Pollok, South Pollok, North Pollok, Priesthill, Craigbank and South Nitshill (postwar.)

The Craigbank scheme was started in 1950. It was comprised of 560 two- and three-storey tenements, of which 176 were three-apartment flats and 384 were four-apartment flats. This was an increase of 228 from the original plan. What was unique about Craigbank was that it contained an experimental district central heating scheme. This obviously had an effect on rents; Craigbank rents were very high. The weekly charge, including rent, heating and rates, for a three-apartment house in Craigbank was £1.6.7d., and a four-apartment £1.12.8d.[3] In the early 1950s in Glasgow, this was a great deal of money. These rents were nearly twice those of the most expensive interwar 'Ordinary' schemes. As a contemporary comment by the Govan Workers' Housing Association had it:

> Very few working people would be wealthy enough to take advantage of the new facilities. The costs were prohibitive, for every shilling in rent there was another shilling added for heating and water.[4]

And a local Bailie (magistrate) said:

> The fact was that very few working people could afford such rents and charges and only a Tory Town Council would ask such rents.[5]

These comments are not quite accurate, as we shall see. There were workers who *were* Craigbank tenants, but these were uniformly well-paid workers – the 'affluent workers' of the 1950s.[6]

Tenanting

The occupational and housing background of pioneer Craigbank tenants was quite varied. Our first tenant to be quoted was something unusual – not unique, but somewhat unusual – in a postwar Glasgow housing scheme: a working-class Tory. Mrs L is a highly articulate, intelligent and versatile person, full of initiative, a wartime Personnel Officer and Welfare Supervisor in a big engineering firm. Her husband was a highly paid consultant metallurgist and foundryman whose work involved much travel. They had two children. Even relatively high earners like these found housing a problem in postwar Glasgow:

> Mrs L: Before we got the [council] house, we were staying in Wilton Gardens for a while . . . Our friend's flat was sub-let to us, we got the five-apartment flat. Well, what was it? About £3 a week.

Mrs L had put her name on the council housing list immediately when she got married in 1945.

Mr F was a charge-hand in the licensing trade, meaning that he managed pubs owned by someone else. This was well-paid work.

> Mr F: As a charge-hand, I was earning £7 per week.
> SD: That was good wages in those days?
> Mr F: That was very good wages.

But again, the housing situation constrained even Mr F – and his wife, who earned £2.10.0d per week as a sales assistant – in poor conditions:

> Mr F: Her [his wife's] mother was a great one in the Cooperative . . . She knew all the big shots and that in the Cooperative and she got us a house in Gloucester Square, a two-room-and-kitchen. In Tradeston. Without a word of a lie, I had to line the whole of the skirting-boards with tin to keep the rats from coming through, and we were three [floors] up . . . The weekly rent was roughly three pounds.

They too put their name on the council housing list when they got married:

> Mr F: Well to be truthful with you, when we got married at first, my wife put in an application for a council house. Now we didn't get offered this house until 1951 and we had been married since 1934. That was eighteen years Bella said we had waited for a house.

Mr C was a time-served foreman marine engineer in the shipbuilding industry. This couple and their three young children also had their housing problems:

> Mr C: I was staying in Cartside Street, in a bigger house, a two-room-and-kitchen, inside toilet and bath, the usual, but, it had black smoke. I was doing a lot of nightshift and quite often my wife would say, she would open the door, she was in to waken me up in the afternoon and the place was full of smoke. So that was when she started to push the Corporation. Before that she had just put her name down and forgotten about it. So when she got this condition in the house she started to push them about it.

SD: How did she push them? Can you remember?

Mr C: Just going in and pestering them. She got hold of her local councillor. Her friends always said, 'You weren't afraid of going to your Town Councillor.' She pushed the case as it were.

In passing, Mrs C was neither the first nor the last in a long line of *women* who took the initiative in agitating for a tenancy, as we have seen in other schemes. There were others who were in inadequate private rented accommodation in the city's West End:

SD: What did you do after the war?

Mr T: I became a taxi-driver, then I bought a taxi and I became a taxi-owner. My wife became pregnant and we managed to get a requisitioned house in Byres Road, and there were three families in it. We had two rooms and we shared the kitchen. There was no bathroom, just a toilet.

He too agitated for a council house.

Mr T: Well, I used to go to the housing place in the Trongate every week.

SD: Looking for a house?

Mr T: Looking for a house. I always went up there and I kept my name in front of them because I was desperate for a house. They said, 'Would I go to Pollok?' At that time I had a taxi and I said, 'I'll go anywhere so long as it is decent and if it is OK.'

Mrs McD and her husband worked in Barr and Stroud's optical engineering factory in Anniesland. They too lived in private rented accommodation in Otago Street in the West End.

SD: What kind of property was that? What kind of accommodation did you have there?

Mrs McD: A big room and the use of a kitchenette, and there was a bathroom next door.

SD: Can you remember what you were paying there in rent? Roughly?

Mrs McD: £1.10.0d a week. And there was a gas meter.

Impressions of the new scheme varied, but were largely very positive. Mrs L, quoted above, would have preferred to be a member of the

Property-Owning Democracy, but the Corporation made her an offer she could not refuse.

> Mrs L: Well I would rather have had a non-Corporation house, not that I'm a snob, but I've seen what happens to Corporation property that's improperly factored . . . I went down, and she [the clerk] said, 'I believe you're interested in a house in Craigbank.' I said, 'A house, any house, as long as it's in a decent area.' And I'd already looked at the map and there was an avenue of trees where this house was, and nobody was looking into me and there was a field at the back which wouldn't be built on, and I thought well, to hell, a house is a house, so I took the house, and I went out.

Others were much more enthusiastic.

> SD: What was it actually like coming into the house through the door on the first day?
>
> Mrs T: I just thought it was heaven. It was wonderful, and I just never thought that I could have such a lovely place. The comfort and the facilities, everything was just wonderful. Nice surroundings that was all I could ever wish for. It was lovely!

And:

> SD: What was the experience of opening the door and looking at the scheme and looking at the house?
>
> Mr C: I was just off the nightshift and I wanted my bed. It was a cold, wet, sleety, snowing morning and I was freezing. I came in here and I felt the heat, in these days it was heat, it was good. There was a cabinet in that corner there and I just sat on the cabinet, turned round and put my feet across there, put my head back and went to sleep. I was dead beat, I was out for the count. I was doing about a twelve-hour nightshift and I had had enough.

The heating was mentioned by many other tenants:

> Mr T: So he [the Housing Department clerk] said, 'There you are, go out and have a look at this area first of all and see what you think.' The two of us came out one night and we had a look at the place – it was dark. It was

only being built at that time, but that part was finished up right enough, this whole block. We went across the road to a part that was occupied, and asked the one up [the tenant] there if they would let us see the house that we had been offered. So they took us in, and oh, right away, there was heating and everything – oh aye, this is it.

Because of the high rents, it soon became plain that the Corporation was checking carefully that future Craigbank tenants were capable of paying them.

Mrs L: Oh, they asked our income and it had to be above £7 per week.

And:

Mr E: My wife's eyes lift up, she just said, 'Oh, can we afford it?' We just had to afford it. The rent and rates was £12 per month.

(Mr E is wrong in his memory of his rent. The monthly charge included rent, rates and heating, and, as we saw on p. 104 was £6.10.8d. per month for a four-apartment house. Nevertheless, this couple were willing to sacrifice to live in a good house in a good scheme.)

And:

Mr T: So we came back and told them and they said, 'You haven't been given the rent.' Now at that time it was in old money. It was 39/- a week, rent, rates and heating. So I thought to myself, well, the heating, and it is marvellous heating. So I said, 'That's all right,' but I had to show a tax return to prove that I could afford it.
SD: Did you?
Mr T: Yes.
SD: You had to show that to the Corporation clerk?
Mr T: Yes.
SD: To the clerk?
Mr T: Yes, to the clerk. I had to prove that I could afford the rent.

And:

SD: What about the rent?
Mrs McM: Well, I knew we could make it – £7.10.0d. a month. I knew we just had to make it!

Mr T: Anybody who came here had to have a good job. I can tell you that most of the people when we came here – there are 530 houses, I think, in this scheme – and I would say that 95 per cent were all like commercial travellers, dozens of policemen and tradesmen.

And:

Mr C: The people in this scheme then were all very steady people. They were all carefully vetted. I only got in here because I was a foreman at that time.

SD: How do you know that?

Mr C: Well they asked me where I worked and what my wages were.

The new houses, however, were not problem-free:

SD: When you first went in the door of that house, what was it like?

Mrs L: Improperly finished trade work, drawers with the remnants of piece-papers and mice dirt. Floorboards under the radiators at the window were spaced like that, which became eventually embarrassing because a couple downstairs were in their bed down below me, you could hear every turn of the bedsprings. But I'd workmen in the house and the Master of Works if he saw me coming he used to hide. I used to go down and say 'I want this done, I want that done.' Wires in the lights had been stuck into the rows of the ceiling and connected to nothing.

SD: No kidding?

Mr L: They just stuck the wires into the rows in the ceilings . . .

Mrs L: They put them in, stuck the knots in to keep the wires from coming out and screwed them on. I mean the things he found in that house you wouldn't believe. You wouldn't believe it.

The flat roofs also caused a lot of problems:

Mr E: The top flat my wife would have liked but, I had been warned about not taking a top flat house because I know the chap who had done the roof, and he said that there would be a lot of trouble and so there has been. The firm that did them were supposed to have put on, I understand, eight layers of felt. When they came to repair them they only found five layers of felt. Of course, I was warned by this certain party, I am not going to mention any names because they are strong business. I was warned on my life not to take a top flat.

SD: Are you implying that the contractors were at it?

Mr E: Oh, they were definitely at it.

SD: How come the Corporation Building Inspectors never found that out? Were they at it too?

Mr E: They must have been!

And:

Mr L: The other thing was the roofs . . .

Mrs L: Oh God aye, the roofs . . . In the bloody ceiling in my daughter's bedroom there was about eight different places where the water was coming in. I ran round with all the buckets, you name it . . .

Mr L: The roofs were – when the sun shone –

Mrs L: – Crack, crack, crack!

Mr L: When the winter came they contracted . . .

Figure 6.1 Prestwick Street, Craigbank, 2004

Mrs L: Well that was one thing about it. That's right, supposed to be three coats or something and he was running out of money and he skimped it on one, and I think it was in the block across the road from us – that was the first one that showed up.

Hardship with the Increased Rent

The substantial increase in rent, not to mention the cost of decorating and furnishing the new house, meant economic hardship for many of the new tenants in Craigbank.

Mr E: Isa's [his wife's] mother said no. She said it was too hefty, that we would never manage it.
SD: The rent, you mean?
Mr E: The rent.
SD: Yes, but you did?
Mr E: We did. We just made a point of it.

And:

SD: When you first came in 1951, how did you do the decorating?
Mr E: A room at a time . . . I will be truthful with you. That carpet in the hall didn't go down till twenty years ago [1971]. We never had a holiday. Everything was tied up with the rents and rates and that. You know what I mean. It was a millstone round our neck.

In the early 1950s Mr E was earning about £9 per week as a bar manager, relatively good wages for the time.

And:

Mrs K: And any overtime Bill had went out into the house. Neither of us smoked, or we couldn't afford to have a drink, and we never drank anyway in those days, and it was a case of everything went on the children and into the house . . . But, on the whole, it was fun just building up your house.
Mrs T: It was all done gradually.

And:

SD: How did you furnish the house?

Mrs McM: Well you couldn't. You see, to let you understand when we came here at first, there was nobody had any carpets . . . The house was covered in the cheap stuff, Congoleum.* You didn't have curtains that came down the full length, or they didn't close, but it didn't matter.

SD: Did you find it difficult to make ends meet?

Mrs McM: Very.

SD: How did you do it?

Mrs McM: Just by watching what we spent. I had Congoleum for years, many years, although Harry had a secure job we didn't push it. We began to get a bit frustrated, but rather than go into debt for anything like that we just did as we could do.

* Congoleum is the brand-name of a form of linoleum.

A lot of DIY was practised in Craigbank by tenants who were tradesmen. The foreman engineer quoted earlier said, when asked about furnishing costs:

Mr C: I made it!

SD: You made it?

Mr C: You don't know me. If I cannae afford it, I made it! I made that table, I made that cabinet and all these wee tables you see lying about here.

A lot of DIY happened in the gardens:

Mr K: I think we were all, being tradesmen or otherwise, at least we could measure and we paced out, measured and divided the square yardage by eight, and then we made out a plan and sort of – hopefully intelligently – apportioned it all out. And then we appointed what we thought would be the drying green area. We marked that out. The Corporation didn't provide any slabs, but we again, we just got together and got the necessary amount of slabs – well, better not say it, falling-off-a-lorry situation! But they were from the workplace we were in.

Tenancy Structures

There was a mix of tenants in Craigbank in terms of occupation, but a difference of opinion as to how this evinced itself. Our working-class Tory put it:

> SD: So you're talking about a group of people who were a mixture of –
>
> Mrs L: – Artisan and professional.
>
> Mr L: Very much a mixture.
>
> Mrs L: There was quite a mix. People owned their own businesses, for instance, and umpteen lived in Craigbank. Small business people. Builders.
>
> Mr L: Gas showroom managers.
>
> Mrs L: Oh there were workers as well. Funnily enough, there was no snobbery in the scheme.
>
> Mr L: You can take it that the manual workers were in it [the scheme] because they wanted out of where they were and they were willing to pay that bit extra to get it. I mean that was the impression I got.

The bar manager had a different impression:

> Mr F: In here? They were quite a lot of snobs. A lot of people who had come from Maryhill and all around about there and thought when they came to Craigbank they were something. Snobby people.

The foreman engineer was also somewhat critical:

> Mr C: The people in Craigbank were inclined to be, eh –
>
> SD: – snobby, would you say?
>
> Mr C: No they weren't snobs, just upstarts. Upstarts as I call them, uppity. They suddenly got into a good scheme and it run away with them. If some people got a home-help they tried to treat her as a servant.

It was as if the tenants of Craigbank were trying to emulate those of pre-war Mosspark.

And Mrs L manages to contradict herself a bit!

> Mrs L: The only thing that suddenly comes into my mind is the fact that the other schemes round about – Priesthill, South Nitshill, part of

> Househillwood – referred to us as the toffs and it was a common expression when we planted our bedding plants out – 'Come on up see what the toffs have planted', and the next day when you got up, your bedding plants werenae there.

Tom Brennan, an early commentator on Glasgow's postwar council housing schemes, states that the tenants of Craigbank were regarded as snobs by other Pollok tenants because they opted to pay the higher rents necessitated by the district heating system.[7] Unfortunately he does not provide any evidence for this allegation. He also notes that there seemed to have been a high turnover of tenants in Craigbank in the 1950s, which could be put down to the high rents. But, he comments:[8]

> . . . it seems more likely that people moved out of Craigbank, and out of Pollok altogether, because they felt themselves to be surrounded by a population not as good as their own.

As again he provides no evidence for this statement, and as the council house card index is completely unreliable for reasons to be dealt with later, this must remain at the level of speculation. However, a modicum of light can be cast upon the inter-scheme relationships within Pollok when we come to consider South Pollok.

Early Community Life

For the pioneer tenants, Craigbank was widely perceived as a good scheme in which to live:

> SD: In the 1950s when you came here, what kind of place was it for kids to grow up in Craigbank?
>
> Mr C: Well you could leave your door open all day. In fact, when you went to bed and forgot to shut it it didn't matter. It was a safe place. I mean, you were never worried. I mean, it was a good area, for me it was a good place to stay. A delightful place. A place where you were proud in a way to bring friends up to your house because the whole place was nice. You got the odd bad one but they never stayed because they suddenly discovered they were out of their own environment.

Mr C. unfortunately did not expand on what a 'bad one' was, but presumably it was someone who was 'undeserving' and definitely not 'respectable'.

And:

> Mr T: The scheme was lovely. We got the phone transferred here because I had to have a phone for the taxi. When the bloke came to install it, he said, 'This is a fantastic scheme.' He had 440 applications for a scheme with 500-odd houses! It was a lovely scheme. Round there at Newfield Place, it was a showpiece. We had tennis courts and a bowling-green . . . This was a marvellous place. A very friendly neighbourhood.

And:

> Mrs McM: We had such a fantastic community. We had a man who worked in the Fruit Market, and he had a whole area out there where he planted gooseberry bushes, raspberry bushes, you name it, and every vegetable imaginable. Oh, he was fantastic! The men took an interest and the gardens were all dug up and the back green was laid by the men, the neighbours, here. We had a very, very caring community. Really absolutely fantastic. If somebody's child was playing out front or something like that, or somebody's child needed a pee-pee, they would get the message and say, 'In', that's the way it was.

Craigbank children were well-behaved and well-policed by local adults, according to the long-term tenants:

> Mr T: The kids were looked after and they weren't allowed to play in the close. No way were they allowed to play in the close – up and down the stair, that was out.
>
> Mrs T: They were disciplined.

And:

> SD: In the 1950s did your children, when they were young, play outside in the street, in the neighbourhood?
>
> Mr E: Yes.
>
> SD: Did that cause any problems at all?
>
> Mr E: Not at all. There were seventeen children in these twelve houses.

SD: So there were a lot of kids about?

Mr E: Seventeen, I am telling you.

SD: And that didn't cause any problems?

Mr E: No animosity at all.

The organisational ability of the Craigbank tenants was critically reflected in the local Tenants' Association. This was formed early on in the life of the scheme. The first tenants arrived in Craigbank in late 1950. By the summer of the next year, the Tenants' Association had taken Glasgow Corporation to court. The issue was the central heating system – or, as the forceful Mrs L insisted, background heating:

SD: What about the central heating?

Mrs L: Not central heating, background heating.

SD: I beg your pardon?

Mrs L: Now there's a clear difference. They only guarantee to give you a temperature of 60 or something, but any heat further than that – that was high enough for a bedroom but any heat further than that you had to supply it yourself. And –

Mr L: – Depended on where your house was. Some houses were at 80 [degrees Fahrenheit], you were wiping the sweat off. Other houses were freezing.

SD: This would depend on nearness to District Heating System?

Mr L: I presume so, yes.

The heating issue is in fact remembered in considerable detail:

Mrs B: Well, the first year we were here, we came in and the heating was put off and the Craigbank tenants were against this. When they contacted the Housing Department, they were told that it would go off from May to September to allow them to clean the boiler up there, but we still had to pay the same rent. So people thought that because we didn't have the heating, the rent should have been reduced. Either that or the heating is kept on. So there were two men, a Mr Knox and I can't remember the other man, went as test cases and fought it in Edinburgh.

And:

SD: Now, let's see what we can remember about this. The tenants' case was that the heating went off from April to September and that it was needed –
Mr L: – No, the tenants' case was that there was nothing said in the lease that the heating could go off and –
SD: And that the heating was paid for per month?
Mrs L: Yeah – it was split over 12 months.
SD: And the Corporation's case was that it didn't matter, that that was the deal anyway?
Mr L: The Corporation's case was that the heating in all public buildings goes off at a certain date, and comes back on at a certain date – which is the same thing that happens today.
Mrs L: But a house is not a public building.
SD: The way we read this is that we found a report on the case in the *Glasgow Herald* in 1952, which means that the case was taken very soon after the scheme was first tenanted. Now it went to an Interim Interdict, the Corporation caved in –
Mrs L: – we got an Interdict against them, that's right.
SD: And then the Corporation pulled a smart trick and rejigged all the leases?
Mrs L: That's right, that's what happened.
SD: To make them be correct in the letter of the law, not in the spirit.
Mrs L: Cause it never went to proof, you know in court.

The *Glasgow Herald* report in question read:

'GLASGOW RESTORES SPACE HEATING.
TENANTS' LEGAL ACTION.'[9]

Glasgow Corporation are [sic] to restore the space heating they withdrew from the housing scheme at Craigbank, Househillwood, on June 25, as a result of legal action taken by about 400 of the tenants concerned, it was stated yesterday, when the case came before Sheriff N. M. L. Walker for interdict. Interim interdict had already been granted previously by Sheriff Inglis on the application of the tenants. Mr George Kirkland, for the Town Clerk's Department said yesterday that immediate steps were being taken

> to restore the heating, following consultation with the responsible department. On this undertaking being given, the interim interdict was recalled.
>
> On behalf of the pursuers, Mr J. Campbell Sewell, solicitor, said that the action was taken at the insistence of the local tenants' association whose membership comprised 400 of the 560 tenants of the scheme. Some of the houses were of the luxury type in respect of which rents were very high.

In terms of their well-developed sense of their own dignity and respectability, the Craigbank Tenants' Association resembled that in Mosspark. They were not prepared to be bullied by the 'Fascists' in the Corporation.

Am. Dram.

The voluntary organisation which perhaps typifies Craigbank more than any other was the scheme's amateur dramatic society, the Craigbank Players. This society performed plays by Joe Corrie, the Scottish working-class dramatist, J. B. Priestley, Sean O'Casey and Aldous Huxley, inter alia – an impressive range. Like many amateur dramatic societies, the Craigbank Players had the odd prima donna:

> Mrs L: . . . there were some quite good players in it. I didn't play much in it because as chairman I felt you should sit back and let other people get a chance. And there was another lady in it who will remain nameless, all her renderings were very histrionic and they wanted me to double up with her and do it night in, night out. No way!

The histrionic lady in question said:

> Mrs McM: Quite a lot of us joined the Drama Club. We could have got more, but they were a wee bit kind of shy about performing in front of other people, or making a fool of themselves. We had a very successful Drama Club. We won festivals at the Pollok Centre.
>
> SD: Roughly how many people were involved in the Drama Club?
>
> Mrs McM: I would say about thirty-six.

Craigbank also ran its own newsletter, the *Craigbank Bulletin* – 'The official organ of the Craigbank Tenants' Association'– although such newsletters were known elsewhere in Glasgow. Not surprisingly, the formidable Mrs L was heavily involved.

> Mrs L: I was editor of the Craigbank Bulletin for a long time! We wrote it!
> Mr L: We wrote the bloody thing!
> SD: That's interesting. So you had a local newspaper?
> Mrs L: It was a small booklet, sort of. About 8 by 5 or something.
> SD: Right. And that came out how often?
> Mrs L: Once a month. And you got hatches, matches and dispatches and all the usual letters to the Editor, sometimes recipes, and by that time I'd been travelling a lot in France with my husband and I was always interested in cooking and I used to bring in the odd French recipe that was simple to make – but there was all sorts of things in it.

There was one aspect of life in Craigbank which was highly unsatisfactory, and to which practically every tenant referred, and that was the sound insulation. In Scotland, this is known as 'deafening':

> Mrs L: The queer thing was, you could be sitting in the house, two floors up, and hear a piano playing, you'd swear blind it was through the wall. It was in the next close on the ground floor. You know the way the sound travelled but the deafening was never put in properly.

And:

> Mrs L: Generally it was a fairly happy place apart from Craigbank neurosis. To explain that one, there was a young doctor moved into the scheme who was a friend of my own doctor who was a personal friend, and my doctor asked me if I'd give him – to get him settled in, and I went with this doctor and acted as his receptionist for a wee while, trained a receptionist for him and he kept getting called out to people, getting these nerve attacks and he'd say, 'Jesus Christ, bloody Craigbank neurosis.' I says, 'What's the matter?' He says, 'No bloody deafening.' They got to the stage where they couldn't stand the noise. You didn't know living in a house it was as bad as that until the folk down below you came up and told you.

Summary

To sum up: Craigbank, as an immediate postwar housing scheme frequently referred to as 'élite' by long-term tenants, invites comparison with Mosspark – an élite interwar scheme. Comparing the social profiles of the two schemes is instructive: precisely the same proportion of tenants – 16 per cent – were in professional occupations. But 59 per cent of Mosspark tenants were white-collar workers as opposed to 22 per cent in Craigbank. And there were 33 per cent skilled manual workers in Craigbank compared with 18 per cent in Mosspark. And no unskilled manual workers appeared in our sample for either scheme. So, to shorthand the similarities and differences, both schemes had a significant proportion of professionals, Mosspark had slightly more than twice the number of white-collar workers than Craigbank, while the latter had slightly less than twice the skilled manual workers than the former. While the presence of a sizeable population of professionals and white-collar workers ensured flourishing voluntary associations of a 'middle-class' nature in both schemes, the presence of a sizeable proportion of manual workers in Craigbank equally ensured that its status was considerably more proletarian than Mosspark's. The houses in Craigbank were exactly the same kind of tenements as elsewhere in Pollok; the difference lay in the central heating. This necessitated the careful selection of a fairly broad spectrum of tenants who shared one central characteristic: they were in *regular* well-paid employment. It was this important attribute which distinguished them from the tenants of the adjoining Priesthill scheme – and, indeed, all other tenants in postwar Pollok. But this distinction in status was perceived by both locals and outsiders as a very real one. Craigbank tenants made all this perfectly clear:

> SD: What do you think the Corporation wanted in Craigbank when you came here? What do you think the Corporation was trying to do with people like yourselves?
>
> Mr C: Well, I think the Labour Party had a wee bit bigger ideas than they should have, maybe. They forgot about human nature. They wanted to give the worker a better life. They didn't see why a worker shouldn't have a central-heated house . . . You see, this is only a standard corporation tenement with central heating. It is not a luxury scheme as some people

like to think it is. It is an 'Ordinary' one with a wee bit of humanity added to it . . . Now when that happens, everybody who came in here – human nature took over, and they suddenly became, 'I live in a centrally heated house you know. I live in Craigbank.' They even talked better!

Be that as it may, for the vast majority of original tenants their first couple of decades in Craigbank were absolute paradise:

Mrs L: I wouldn't say that Craigbank was an 'Ordinary' scheme. It was an extra-ordinary scheme! I mean, there was no typical tenant. You'd everything from a labourer to a manager to an owner. You'd everything in the scheme! Excellent neighbours. I met some really fine people in Craigbank that are still my friends.

In fact, there were no labourers in Craigbank. The neighbour Mrs L *thought* was a labourer, was in fact a shipwright!

And:

Mr T: Brilliant! I thought this was the greatest –

Mrs T: – I thought it was heaven! I mean, you couldn't have had a more comfortable home.

Mr T: Up to 1960 it was very obvious that Craigbank was a super scheme. There were dozens of police in it and I mean dozens – all lived here. It was a very good class of people that was in it. Obviously, it was a scheme that people wanted to get into.

And:

Mrs McM: It was great! The door was never closed. It was just absolutely delightful!

The hidden injuries of sudden class mobility are, however, all too evident in the comment of the bar manager quoted earlier:

SD: Supposing you were to try and sum up your experience of living in Craigbank in the 1950s and 1960s, when your children were growing up, how would you sum it up?

Mr F: The biggest mistake I ever made in my life!

SD: Why do you say that?

Mr F: Well, I have always been short of money, short of money.

SD: Was it too expensive living here?

Mr F: Well, I think so, it was a drain on you.[10]

Nevertheless, Glasgow working-class culture flourished in Craigbank in a way it never did in Mosspark. This was made plain on Hogmanay:

> Mr C: That was just one long boozing session! As long as the drink was there, it was going. You never knew where – you just listened to see where it was at the time. You moved about the stair and everywhere.

And:

> Mr T: Och, you were in every house in the close, and the next close, and the one after that! Singing and dancing – it went on for days!

These New Year celebrations provide a clue to an important fact about Craigbank. Whatever its élite or 'snobby' reputation within Pollok, it was still an overwhelmingly, if not totally, working-class scheme, with a continuity of cultural tradition. Although they sometimes forgot it during their amateur dramatics, its residents were council tenants who, with the possible exception of Mrs L, showed no burning desire to join the property-owning democracy.

Table 6.1 Craigbank occupational structure, 1951

% by row	Professional	White-collar	Managerial	Self-employed	Supervisory	Skilled manual
	16	22	7	4	7	33

Notes

NB: All references preceded by 'GCA' refer to the Glasgow City Archives.

1. Mooney, G. (1988), *Living on the Periphery: Housing, Industrial Change and the State*, PhD Thesis, University of Glasgow, pp. 129ff.
2. Ibid.
3. GCA: Corporation of Glasgow City Factor's Department: *Letting Regulations and General Notes on the Scheme of Allocation in Operation as at 31st March, 1951*, p. 19; *Govan Press*, 29, 12, 50.
4. Quoted in Mooney (1988), op. cit., p. 26.

5. Ibid., p. 27.
6. See Goldthorpe, J., D. Lockwood, F. Bechhofer and J. Platt (1969), *The Affluent Worker in the Class Structure*, Cambridge University Press, for an extended discussion of this term.
7. Brennan, T. (1959): *Reshaping a City*, House of Grant, p. 235.
8. Ibid., p. 151.
9. *Glasgow Herald*, 18 July 1951.
10. I take the term from Sennett, R. and J. Cobb (1993), *The Hidden Injuries of Class*, New York: Knopf.

7

South Pollok: 'The Bundy'

Development of South Pollok

South Pollok was a very small scheme developed in 1947–8 in a space at the Peat Road roundabout, north of Priesthill and south of the well-planned, pre-war 'Old' Pollok scheme. It was a stopgap site, originally earmarked for social and leisure facilities.[1] Built under the provisions of the 1946 Housing Act, it was categorised as an 'Intermediate' scheme, thus ensuring continuity of the pre-war three-tier system, although it was unique in the Pollok area. It comprised the following streets: Bridgend Road, Cowglen Road, Dykefoot Drive, Fairhill Avenue, Lawside Drive, Linnbank Avenue and Nerston Road. It consisted of 226 houses, of which 132 were in three-storey tenements, 6 were semi-detached cottages, 12 were terraced tenements and 76 were two-storey flats. Of this stock, the tenements were the last to be built, and were the houses which bounded the Barrhead Road. All of these houses were either three- or four-apartment. The rents in South Pollok were considerably lower than in adjoining Priesthill. The annual rental for a three-apartment house was £17.10.0d., and for a four-apartment £20.5.0d.

For reasons which are obscure, but are probably to do with sheer demand from poorer tenants, the scheme was used substantially for housing overcrowded tenants from slum areas on Glasgow's south side, such as the Gorbals and Govan. Mooney states that over 130 of the original 226 tenants came from these areas.[2] This, coupled with its flat-roofed tenemental design, shocked the adjacent tenants in 'Old' Pollok in exactly the same manner as West Drumoyne did the tenants of the 'Ordinary' Drumoyne scheme, as we have seen above. South Pollok had a short life; it was demolished in 1973 to make way for the Pollok shopping centre. But it is included in this book to demonstrate that within one general council housing area – Greater Pollok – it was possible to have two such divergent schemes as Craigbank and South Pollok. It is curious that the Corporation persisted in developing schemes with such marked distinctions in quality and character in the postwar years, when it was obvious that this would exacerbate tension between the tenants. After all, it had the experience of Blackhill and Riddrie upon which to draw. It seems that officials must have been total prisoners of their own ideology about who was and was not 'deserving'.

Tenanting South Pollok

A methodological note is necessary here: it proved very difficult to trace original tenants from this scheme. The following extracts are from two interviews with one extended family. The first involved an elderly lady (Mrs B Snr) of 78 who was such a tenant, along with her 58-year-old son (Mr B) and a procession of her married daughters. Mrs B Snr was in bed unwell during this interview and her daughters were looking after her. All family members contributed to this interview. The second interview was with Mr B and his wife, the daughter of Mrs B Snr – designated Mrs B Jnr. At the time of the interviews, both sets of interviewees lived in the good-quality, interwar 'Old' Pollok scheme. (The significance of this will be evident in the text.) Mrs B Snr believed she was the only original tenant of South Pollok left alive:

> Mrs B Snr: You see, most of the old South Pollok people are a' dead. Most of my old neighbours are a' dead.

The origins of the pioneer tenants of South Pollok were in various locations of small poor-quality houses mainly on the south side of the city (that is, south of the River Clyde), with a large proportion coming from the Gorbals. The pattern of removal of the original tenants into the new scheme was random, unlike that of the interwar 'Slum-Clearance' schemes. Mrs B Snr makes this plain:

> SD: I mean, like when you came out here, were there a lot of your neighbours came with you, Mrs B?
>
> Mrs B Snr: No, I was the only one.

Mrs B Snr had lived with seven children in a room-and-kitchen tenement flat in Kinning Park, sharing an outside toilet with four other flats. She had been on the Corporation housing list for fourteen or fifteen years. Her husband was a seaman who was away from home most of the time.

> SD: Can you remember how much your husband was earning per week?
>
> Mrs B Snr: Very little!
>
> Mr B: Seaman's wages.
>
> Mrs B Snr: It was very little. It was monthly. It was very, very little.
>
> Mr B: Not much. It wasnae much. A monthly allotment.

The social and occupational profiles of the original South Pollok tenants – remembering that it was classified as an 'Intermediate' scheme – are practically identical to those of interwar 'Slum-Clearance' schemes. But as contemporary slum-clearees were also being rehoused in Priesthill, in line with general postwar housing policy, the most plausible explanation for these anomalous profiles is that South Pollok was reserved unofficially by the Housing Department for the poorest of the poor. It may be that the name was changed in an effort to avoid the stigma attached to the 'Rehousing' label, but no evidence was found for this hypothesis. Mrs B Snr and her family were certainly in this category – as were neighbours.

> SD: What were your neighbours like, Mrs B Snr? What kind of people were they?
>
> Mrs B Snr: Oh, good down-to-earth people. Good people. Poor. But good. Most of them were dockers.

It is worth emphasising that, as Young and Wilmott were discovering in contemporary Bethnal Green, docking was a notoriously seasonal and low-paid occupation in an alleged era of affluence,[3] a phenomenon Gareth Stedman Jones showed was the case decades earlier in Victorian London,[4] and James Treble equally demonstrated for pre-1914 Clydeside.[5]

A final vital social characteristic of the pioneer tenants of South Pollok is that 26 per cent of them were 'TB cases'.[6] This fact rapidly led to South Pollok acquiring the nickname of 'The White Man's Graveyard', the first of two pejorative labels attached to the scheme; the contemporary social stigma attached to TB should not be underestimated. The second and more enduring nickname was 'The Bundy'. This derived from the 'Bundy' punch-clock at the tram-terminus at the Peat Road/Househillwood roundabout. In Glasgow gangland rhetoric, it also stands for 'Boys United Never Die Young!'

Impressions of the New Scheme

South Pollok was as much appreciated by its first tenants as any other new Glasgow housing scheme.

> SD: So, can you remember coming out to South Pollok and looking at that house?
>
> Mrs B Snr: Uh-huh.
>
> SD: What was it like?
>
> Mrs B Snr: It was like heaven! It was like a palace, even without anything in it . . . We'd got this lovely, lovely house. Well it was lovely to me! When I got into that big empty house and the weans were running up and doon mad and – it was just like walking into Buckingham Palace because I had a bath!
>
> Mr B: Electric light and all.
>
> Mrs B Snr: Electric light! The weans did nothing but switch it on and off –
>
> Mr B: – And then a bath! I mean that was a –
>
> Mrs B Snr: – It was an achievement for the likes of us, you know, because as I say, I was brought up in the Gorbals and I mean that was slums, really slums, but anyway, when I got to the Bundy, I thought I'd landed lucky.

This statement demonstrates that Mrs B Snr had internalised the negative discourse on the nature of the Gorbals.

Given the low and irregular income of many of the original tenants, decorating and furnishing the new, big houses was a problem. (Mrs B Snr's house had four apartments.)

> SD: How did you furnish a big house like that?
>
> Mrs B Snr: We just lay on the floor!
>
> Mr B: We did lie on the floor, bought mattresses.
>
> Mrs B Snr: We did – we bought mattresses first, and lay on the floor. And then we eventually – there were nae free handouts in they days. You got

– you eventually bought maybe a bit of second-hand furniture. But you managed eventually. But it was wooden boards for a long time.

As in other schemes with a similar tenants' occupational profile, for example Blackhill and Hamiltonhill, 'The Bundy' was experienced as a scheme of good neighbours and self-entertainment:

Mrs B Snr: Well, they always had trips for the wee ones, and concerts in the backs – because Maggie [her daughter] was in all the concerts, singing' and dancin' concerts.

SD: So these concerts that were put on were for your own entertainment, for the people in the scheme?

Mrs B Snr: Oh aye, aye.

SD: Did you do it outdoors in the good weather?

Mrs B Snr: We would do it in the back-green in the good weather.

SD: Were they like the old-fashioned clabbers? Would you call them clabbers?

Mrs B Snr: Well I would have called them clabbers. Just social getting-together and having singing or dancing, out in the back. Mind they charged you a penny or a ha'penny.

However, it did not take long for the new tenants to discover that their flats were poorly constructed, and Mooney notes a litany of complaints about this, and also endemic damp.[7] Following the situation in Hamiltonhill and Blackhill, the pioneer tenants were of a similar demographic: young, growing families. One of Mooney's respondents commented insightfully about South Pollok:

One of the problems with that wee scheme was that there were too many people in it. The density was too high for the size of the place.[8]

The 'Bundy' Stigma

Within a few years of its construction, South Pollok was a uniquely stigmatised scheme within the Pollok area. There seem to have been three elements in the social construction of this stigma: (i) the existence of a youth gang in the scheme; (ii) the attitudes towards it of tenants of *older* Pollok schemes like 'Old' Pollok and Househillwood; and (iii) the construction of highly visible council *tenements* along the main Barrhead Road about a year after the original part of the scheme was finished. Mrs B Snr and her son discuss these elements:

> SD: Outsiders frequently say that the Bundy was different because it had a gang?
>
> Mrs B Snr: Och aye! He [her son] was one of them! Do you know what they run about wi'?
>
> SD: What?
>
> Mrs B Snr: Toy guns that my man brought frae Canada and America, wi' him being a seaman. He used to bring them toy guns and suede shirts wi' –
>
> Mr B: – Replica guns.
>
> Mrs B Snr: Replica. And the other kids used to say, 'Oh James Baxter's got a real gun. His daddy brought it from America! That was – it was only kids' stuff.
>
> SD: Were you in this gang, Mr Baxter?
>
> Mr B: Oh aye.
>
> Mrs B Snr: Aye, he was – he was just a wild boy like the rest!

In a subsequent interview with Mr B Jnr and his wife, the gang was discussed further:

> Mr B: Och, it was just one bunch of young boys against another yin, you know, another young team, nothing very serious in it. A few sore faces handed out, you know.
>
> Mrs B Jnr: Definitely was. They were called the Bundy Boys, it's no use kiddin' and swankin', they were.

It should be noted that Mr B is referring to the late 1940s/early 1950s. He was away for two years in the mid-fifties doing his National Service, and was no longer interested in gangs when he returned home. But, in the Byzantine system of Glasgow gangs, the younger boys in the scheme had already adopted the mantle of the gang:

> Mr B: You got a' the wee ones that were only this size, by the time the gang was ready for breaking up, they declared themselves the Bundy Boys –

Mrs B Jnr: – they declared themselves the Bundy Boys –

Mr B: – and the name –

Mrs B Jnr: – the name carried on.

Mr B: But it was just a name. The original Bundy Boys at that time were all in the Army because you had National Service.

But personnel apart, the persistence of the gang in one form or another into the 1960s, not to mention the existence of pistols, real or replica, ensured that the stigma of the scheme continued. It was powerful enough for young locals to camouflage their place of residence when consorting with other young Glaswegians – a phenomenon which has been noted elsewhere as a characteristic of stigmatised housing schemes.[9]

Mrs B Jnr: And it used to be if anybody asked where you came frae, you didnae say the Bundy, you just said Pollok. No way – 'I'm no lettin' them know I came frae the Bundy', in case you were classed with the gang.

The legend of the gang was very powerful in the Pollok area, and well-known elsewhere in Glasgow, particularly on the South Side. It was strong enough to be featured in the maps of Glasgow gangland supplied with the notorious 1973 book, *A Glasgow Gang Observed.*[10] But according to some locals reminiscing on the 'My Pollok' blogspot on the Internet, the violence was real enough.

molbiol194 said:

> I lived in the 'Bundy' scheme and had a great time. I remember however I saw a sword fight outside my front window when I was about nine. It scared the shit out of me! Also another time a taxi-driver and a local Ned had a knife fight outside my window. I had a fight every couple of months and even started to enjoy them. You had to stand up for yourself. [6 December 2013, accessed 25 July 2017]

And the convenor of the 'blueskyscotland' site about Pollok replied:

> Hi Molbiol194
> I used to go to school beside the original Bundy, like everyone else in Pollok as both schools were right next to it, and it definitely had a reputation as

> the area with the toughest gang at that time [1950s to 1970s]. [7 December 2013, accessed 25 July 2017]

So, as with all Glasgow gangs, it is wise not be too romantic about them.

A final point on the Bundy Boys gang is worth making. Replica pistols were unknown in Glasgow in the late 1940s/early 1950s. The existence of even a few of those – always remembering that they are meant to look like the real thing – would accord the gang an incredible notoriety in contemporary Glasgow.

The Attitude of Older Pollok Schemes

In a nutshell, South Pollok was regarded by the adjacent 'Ordinary' interwar scheme of 'Old' Pollok with horror. (It is to be remembered that this interview was being conducted in Mrs B Snr's *current* house in Old Pollok.)

> SD: What were the differences?
> Mrs B Snr: Snobs!
> SD: Did they look down on you?
> Mrs B Snr: Oh definitely.
> Mr B: Oh aye.
> SD: How did you know that?
> Mrs B Snr: Their attitude, you were just a piece of dirt.
> Mr B: If you walked over this way, they followed you.
> Mrs B Snr: To find out what you were up to.
> Mr B: Yeah.

And:

> Mrs B Snr: It was just something about the Old Pollok – if you were an Old Pollok tenant –
> Mr B: – Very much sought after –
> Mrs B Snr: – They were a class on their own. They did nod to you or that, you know, if they got to know you. But very few ever got to know you! I don't think they wanted to know, whether you were – I don't know, people have always looked down on poor people, I don't care what anybody says. It's still going on.

Figure 7.1 Fairhill Avenue, South Pollok, c. 1950

These are important statements providing yet more evidence to support the contention that the proximity of a *higher* status scheme can be an important factor in the amplification of the deviant reputation of stigmatised schemes, as in the proximity of Riddrie to Blackhill, for example. But more importantly, such statements show the dominant ideology that poverty was the fault of the individual was deeply embedded in the contemporary Glaswegian working class. The hard-working 'respectables' may have discriminated symbolically against the poor, and asserted their moral superiority, but they also knew from bitter experience that the loss of a job, or industrial injury, could land them in the same position very quickly. This is why the alleged social distance between the 'deserving' and 'undeserving' poor keeps rearing its head. The former do not want to acknowledge the similarities; they want to believe that they are inherently different from those who live in 'Rehousing' schemes.

The South Pollok Tenements

The B family also felt that the construction of an additional two rows of tenement houses along the busy Barrhead Road about one year after the original construction of the scheme contributed to its stigma. The point was that these houses, and their tenants, were highly *visible* from the main road.

Mrs B Snr: But what spoiled the Bundy was putting the tenements up.

SD: Was there any difference between the tenants of the tenements and yourselves? Were they the same kind of people?

Mrs B Snr: Well I think – no, they were different. See when the tenements got built and the people came in, they were entirely different people.

Mr B: I mean, on the Barrhead Road, there was a guy in particular. There was a porthole window in the kitchens. And there was a boiler, a closed boiler, below the porthole window, you know, next to the sinks. And he was actually selling chips out the porthole window!

SD: He was making them in the boiler?

Mr B: In the boiler. But I mean that's the kind of people that were moving into the tenements.

Mrs B Snr: They seemed to put in worse and worse, if you know what I mean. The class seemed to go lower.

This demonstrates a narrative common to housing schemes – that it was the later tenants who caused their decline and fall.

That there was a negative perception of council *tenements* in Glasgow is borne out by the experience of West Drumoyne, discussed earlier. Be that as it may, the stigma attached to 'The Bundy' did not seem to inhibit its tenants from success in life.

Mrs B Snr: The people and what happened to them, well, as far as I know, made good, haven't they? I mean most of the people that I've heard about, they've never ever looked back, that lived at the Bundy. Every one o' us seemed to go forward, so I mean it wasnae a stigma or anything, to have been living at the Bundy. It was just a name that it got.

Mr B: It's just got a bad name.

Mrs B Snr: Like the Gorbals – it got a name and a' and it stuck to it.

This demonstrates that not only tenants were aware of the existence of stigmatised schemes and neighbourhoods, but also that it didn't matter what they did or didn't do; the damage is already done.

Satisfaction with South Pollok

This extended family *loved* 'The Bundy':

> Mrs B Snr: Oh it was a good place, there's nae two ways about that. Oh, they were good houses. They were really good houses. And, as I say, they were good people. Rough, certainly rough, but I never found any fault with them and they would help you if they could help you. See the likes of me lying in my bed like this noo, I wouldnae need to lay here myself, wouldn't I not – if I'd 'a stayed at the Bundy?
>
> Mr B: No, there'd be somebody here.
>
> Mrs B Snr: There'd have been somebody here night and day.
>
> Mr B: Somebody to go to the messages or various other things. Good neighbours.
>
> Mrs B Snr: Good people.

And:

> SD: So if you were trying to sum up your twenty-odd years in the Bundy in your own words, how would you describe it?
>
> Mrs B Snr: Good. I was quite happy at the Bundy. I had a happy, happy life at the Bundy. I wouldnae say anything different.
>
> Mr B: When I got my mutual exchange back into the Bundy again, I was over the moon – I was delighted.

And:

> Mrs B Jnr: All the years we've lived here, you just couldnae fault it.

Summary

South Pollok was an unusual scheme, an anomaly, in the Pollok area. It has proved impossible to unravel the specific reasons for its construction, nor the quite distinct profile of its tenants. In the first sense, it was constructed to fill a small but real spatial gap in the overall Pollok development. In the second sense, it was probably decided to use it to house slum-clearees on a one-off basis. Neither sense helps us understand why it was designated as an 'Intermediate' scheme. On the other hand, *no* postwar scheme was designated as 'Rehousing'. It has been impossible to trace one Corporation official who can unravel this enigma – indeed, they find it as interesting as I do. But its *function* was plain, whatever its official designation: it was to all intents and purposes exactly the same as an interwar 'Rehousing' scheme. It too was an overwhelmingly manual working-class scheme in 1951, with more than half (53 per cent) of its tenants unskilled workers, about a quarter skilled manual (26 per cent) and 17 per cent women. General labouring was the most common occupation, with others working in metals (13 per cent), transport (9 per cent) and engineering (7 per cent).

It is curious that 'The Bundy' became so stigmatised so rapidly. There can be little doubt that the relative poverty of its tenants provides the general explanation, while its proximity to 'Old' Pollok provides the particular explanation. And the poverty was real. In the contemporary indices of deprivation generated by the Royal Scottish Society for the Prevention of Cruelty to Children (RSSPCC) and the Society of Social Service (SOSS), South Pollok scored highest in the whole Pollok area.[11] And in the contemporary climate of Glasgow's gangland, the sight of one apparently real pistol would have sealed its reputational fate. And that reputation within Pollok was evil.[12] Shortly after it became known as 'The White Man's Grave' and then 'The Bundy', it became known as 'South Korea'. And in a situation which is becoming familiar, its tenants were blamed for the poor construction of the scheme *and* the stigma. But like most such reputations for the city's housing schemes, it was totally unwarranted. As the evidence of the B family demonstrates, 'The Bundy' was a hard-working, cheery scheme displaying all the cultural characteristics of the local semi- and unskilled manual working class. That was probably enough to doom it, for many of the immigrants to the other Pollok schemes were only too keen to try and forget that culture – or certain aspects of it.

It will never be known for certain, but it is highly likely that the bad reputation of 'The Bundy' was not unconnected with the decision in 1973 to demolish it entirely to make way for the new Pollok shopping centre – in the same way that the Gorbals became Glasgow's first Comprehensive Redevelopment Area (CDA) and was literally razed to the ground.

Table 7.1 South Pollok occupational structure, 1951

% by column	1951
Skilled manual	26
Semi-skilled	2
Unskilled	53
Women	17

Notes

NB: All references preceded by 'GCA' refer to the Glasgow City Archives.

1. Mooney (1988), op. cit., p. 393.
2. Ibid., p. 30.
3. Young, M. and P. Willmot (2007), *Family and Kinship in East London*, Penguin Books.
4. Jones, G. (1989), *Outcast London: A Study in the Relationship Between Classes in Victorian Society*, Penguin Books.
5. Treble, J. (1978), 'The Market for Unskilled Male Labour in Glasgow, 1891–1914', in McDougall (ed.), op. cit.
6. Brennan (1959), op. cit., p. 177.
7. Mooney (1988), op. cit., p. 256.
8. Ibid., p. 255.
9. Armstrong and Wilson (1973); Damer (1989), op. cit.
10. Patrick (1973), op. cit.
11. Brennan (1959), op. cit., p. 151. The SOSS was the follower of the Victorian Charity Organisation Society.
12. Mooney (1988), op. cit.

8

Alarums and Excursions

The key general question that has to be asked at this juncture is: Why was Glasgow's council housing so dire? So far, this book has indicated how the driver of Glasgow's council housing policy was 'scheming'. In a city whose population growth was so explosive, it faced an enormous problem in how to manage the supply of housing. It did this by deploying moralistic criteria to allocate council housing so that the 'deserving' got the best, and those deemed the 'undeserving' the worst. This distinction was not a scientific one, but an ideological construct which purported to 'solve' the city's housing problem. Tenants got what they 'deserved'. Glasgow's population growth had been so rapid that tenement housing became – quite improperly – isomorphic with slums.

Population Growth

The first part of the answer to the question at the head of this chapter is: population growth. Consider the rate at which the city's population grew.

Table 8.1 Glasgow population increase, 1801–1951

1801	77,385
1811	100,000
1821	147,043
1841	255,650
1851	329,097
1861	395,503
1901	762,000
1911	784,496
1931	1,088,524
1951	1,090,000

Sources: Glasgow Censuses; Maver (2000).

Thus the population quadrupled between 1801 and 1851, doubled between 1851 and 1901, and grew by another 50 per cent between 1901 and 1931. Housing supply never even remotely kept up with demand. The result, as has been shown, was the breakneck erection of jerry-built backlands, and made-down and farmed-out houses, all of which constituted ready-made slums.

Overcrowding

It is hardly surprising that by the beginning of the twentieth century, Glasgow was the most overcrowded city in Britain, not least because of the Scottish tradition of building small, one- or two-roomed houses in the tenements. Glasgow's population density in 1912 – 53 per acre – was significantly greater than Liverpool's – 45 per acre – its 'rival' in terms of overcrowding.[1] Some of this overcrowding assumed grotesque proportions. By the late 1860s, approximately 50,000 people were crammed into the 36 acres in the city centre which the City Improvements Trust (responsible for slum-clearance) controlled, mainly in the Glasgow Cross area.[2] That is a staggering 1,400 persons to the acre. How anything approaching normal family life could be sustained in such conditions is best left to the imagination – although there is no lack of description, not only in the non-fiction reports produced by the officials of the Corporation's Public Health Department and the Minutes of Evidence to the local Housing Commissions quoted earlier, but also in fiction about the period.[3]

Authoritarian Attitudes

The second key to understanding the development of Glasgow's council housing lies, in fact, in attitudes towards slums and their inhabitants, trapped in a vicious cycle of rotten housing, casualised labour, cyclical unemployment and attendant poverty, in the Victorian years. Rodger has summarised this well:

> Scottish middle-class attitudes to unemployment reflected for much of the Victorian years prevailing responses to poverty and urban discipline in general. Intemperance, idleness and moral degeneracy were interpreted as character defects, remediable only through denial of relief and recognition

> that no institutional long-stop existed to cushion the impact of unemployment. Personal revelation and individual resurrection in the biblical sense of rediscovery and rebirth were central pillars in attitudes towards the disadvantaged in Victorian society.[4]

The offensive nature of these authoritarian attitudes is encapsulated in this comment at the beginning of the twentieth century by the then Professor of Political Economy at the University of Glasgow:

> There is no centre of moral deterioration and infection worse than a bad home. The slum dwellers, as a rule, are the rats who carry the plague, and there is not even the compensation that the rats grow fat. They grow diseased and lean, and, unhappily, they become the parents of more diseased and yet leaner rats.[5]

What is important for our purposes is that these attitudes infused the practice of the Glasgow Property Owners & Factors Association (GPOFA), and were reinforced by the similar contemporary ideas of Octavia Hill about the housing management of the poor. These attitudes were incorporated lock, stock and barrel in an elaborated professional ideology with singularly hard moralistic edges in Glasgow when the City Improvements Department was established to manage the first council housing.

Drastic Measures

In turn, this resulted in a battery of measures on the public health front, of which the nocturnal raiding of the small 'ticketed houses' in the slums was the most draconian.[6] This was the procedure introduced by the Glasgow Police Act of 1862 whereby small houses, defined as those containing less than 2,000 cubic feet, were measured up, and a tinplate disk or 'ticket' screwed to the front door specifying the capacity of that house at a scale of 300 cubic feet per person over eight years of age. (Children under eight were counted as half-a-person!) Thereafter, these houses were raided without warning in the middle of the night by Public Health Inspectors, who would prosecute the tenant – not the landlord – if the number of people in the house exceeded the number specified on the ticket. These powers were considered by the Inspectors and the public alike as oppressive, and the ticketed houses as being stigmatised. This whole practice also made its way into the contemporary fiction of Patrick MacGill.[7] The housing problem was considered so serious in contemporary Glasgow that the Corporation and its officials believed such drastic measures were necessary. While in 2018 such measures would be regarded as a gross violation of civil liberties, in actual fact they were commonplace in Glasgow from the mid-Victorian years up until the start of the Second World War. The historian Geoffrey Best remarked on the Calvinist implications of these measures in Scotland in '. . . producing strong authoritarian streaks in public officials'.[8]

The problem which bedevilled Victorian 'experts' on the slums was that they had conflated slum housing and slum residents in a quite illegitimate manner. In Glasgow, the second half of the nineteenth century had seen an explosion in the construction of working-class tenements with only one or two rooms and outside toilets.[9] It had also seen the construction of 'back-lands' in the back-courts of existing tenements, and 'made-down' houses, whereby the rooms in older, larger properties were recycled as individual houses. This resulted in the gross overcrowding problem to which reference has already been made. However, an outcome was that as all, or most, slums were tenements, there was a tendency to perceive all forms of working-class tenements as slums, or potential slums. But the slums also contained the slum-dwellers, who were inevitably blamed for the rotten housing in which they were trapped; the problems were presented as being within the slums rather than within the state policies which created the slums and slum-dwellers in the first place. This ecological fallacy proposed that because the slums were riddled with poverty and disadvantage, they contained only poor individuals and families, and consequently their new rehousing schemes could only be depositories of the poor and disadvantaged. That this was nonsense has been demonstrated by an analysis of the Draft Roll of the 'Wine Alley' scheme, which was shown to have contained skilled, as well as semi-skilled and unskilled, manual workers.[10] In actual historical fact, the slums contained a heterogeneous population in skill terms. What was ignored in the furore about slums was that their owners made a great deal of money out of them. What was also ignored was the existence of commodious, handsome middle-class tenements in, for example, Glasgow's West End or South Side which manifestly were *not* slums.

It was inevitable that this pernicious ideology would overflow into the council housing management practice of Glasgow Corporation, not least because its Public Health Department was heavily involved in policing the slums. Consequently, generations of Glasgow's council housing managers have been imbued with authoritarian attitudes towards, especially, the tenants of tenemental rehousing schemes. If this was not bad enough, the situation was exacerbated by the fact that the Lettings Section of the City Improvements Department was staffed by only six Clerks, three of whom dealt with enquiries and three with offers. This situation persisted throughout our time period, during which there were no female Clerks or Resident Factors, Octavia Hill's strictures to the contrary. (She had insisted that her rent-collectors – prefigurative housing managers – in the slums of Victorian London were women.[11]) The male Clerks at the Department's central office at 20 Trongate were notorious for their supercilious manner; they had immense power, they knew it, and they abused it. A Craigbank woman put it like this:

> Mrs McB: It was terrible. You would go up and they would chew the face off you . . . I came home crying every time I went up there.
>
> SD: Why did they chew your face off when you went up?
>
> Mrs McB: It was just the attitude of the man. They felt – they treated you like dirt. That's the only way I could say it, you know, but it was really terrible the way – you know, to you.

In the everyday life of the Department, these Clerks made it appear that they were doing the public a favour, rather than granting them their rights. In fact, during the course of the research I was struck by the number of retired and long-serving Departmental officials who insisted that their job *was* to get the rent in. Neither compassion nor courtesy was included in their job description.

This historical perspective on tenements and their inhabitants is necessary to understand, firstly, why the Glasgow Moderate Party, the Scottish Board of Health and the tenants of Drumoyne 'Ordinary' scheme were so vehement during the interwar years in their opposition to the construction of the tenemental West Drumoyne 'Intermediate' scheme, and, secondly, why the tenemental houses in the 'Rehousing'/'Slum-Clearance' schemes were perceived with such fear and loathing, as almost pre-stigmatised. It was as if the built form of this housing always carried within it the bacteria – the 'miasma' so beloved by the Victorians[12] – which infected its inhabitants and caused them to slide inexorably into 'moral degeneracy'. We have seen that the highly visible tenemental housing in South Pollok played a major role in its rapid stigmatisation, and how the construction of the Blackhill tenements sent shivers of horror down the spines of the tenants of the adjacent 'South Riddrie' 'Intermediate' and Riddrie 'Ordinary' schemes.

However, it should not be thought that an antipathy to tenements is peculiar to Glasgow. It is in fact common to all large British cities, and the London situation has been described in detail by both Stedman Jones and Jerry White.[13] Further, similar attitudes prevailed in New York City. As Plunz says in his magisterial history of New York housing, 'By 1865, the word "tenement" was a well-established term in the technical vocabulary of housing for the urban poor.'[14] And he quotes an 1880 commentator on housing:

> There are no objections to apartment houses in American cities, except prejudice, and this is stronger in the United States than elsewhere. To Americans it is a question of rank. Anything we term a tenement house is tabooed.[15]

The Stigma

Quite besides the geographical isolation and environmental disadvantage of such tenemental council housing schemes, and the poverty of their tenants, what Wacquant has called a '*suffusive territorial stigma*' became attached to them.[16] And as has been demonstrated conclusively for the tenemental 'Wine Alley' scheme, not to mention Blackhill, once such a stigma is attached, it is virtually impossible to remove it, even decades after the original events which created it are past.[17] It doesn't matter if some tenants do not conform to the offensive stereotypes attached to their scheme, or reject their validity. Once an urban neighbourhood is stigmatised, the stigma has the cultural potential to survive for a long time, while the 'experts' poke around within it to find the final solution to the problem. As Colin Ward has said:

> The moment that housing, a universal human activity, becomes defined as a problem, a housing problems industry is born, with an army of experts,

bureaucrats and researchers, whose existence is a guarantee that the problem won't go away.[18]

This helps explain the bitterness of the local struggle over the form of new housing for tenement-dwellers, and the Moderate Party's refusal to countenance cottage-type council housing for such people, in spite of all the valiant efforts of the ILP to achieve it. Speaking of the interwar years, Glasgow's historian said correctly:[19] 'The polarisation between right and left remained acute . . .'

If capitalism required a section of the population to be more or less permanently confined to the reserve army of labour, and endure fluctuating employment and hence the inability to pay the rent for a decent house, it camouflages this situation ideologically by blaming the poor for the slums in which they are forced to live. And if this population has to be rehoused for public health reasons, it will ensure that it is warehoused in the least eligible housing – for the poor deserve nothing better because of their profligacy and drunkenness. And to ensure that they do not reproduce these evils in the new tenemental council housing schemes, they will be patrolled by a squadron of officials including Resident Factors, Green Ladies and, of course, the Police. This has been demonstrated in this book for both Hamiltonhill and Blackhill. And the sheer scale of these patrols can be gauged by the fact that, in Glasgow, they involved eighty Resident Factors in interwar 'Intermediate' and 'Rehousing' schemes containing 29,641 houses and an estimated (minimum) population of 142,276 people.[20]

What is striking in the data about family and social life in 'Rehousing' schemes in Glasgow in the interwar and immediate postwar years is its Dickensian nature. The elaborate cultural survival mechanisms which the poor of the Victorian and Edwardian eras were forced to construct in order to survive in their slums – thieving, menages, money-lending, hawking, gambling, recycling sugar-bags as bedding, illegal micro-businesses, etc. – were evident until well after the Second World War in such schemes, right up to an era in which the population allegedly 'never had it so good'.[21] In Hamiltonhill, Blackhill and the 'Wine Alley', tenants were reproducing the cultural behaviour of the old Gorbals, or Campbell Bunk or the Seven Dials in London, for this was a national rather than a local phenomenon.[22] The point about these coping strategies is that they were forced upon the poor; they did not construct them for recreation.

The Effects of the Stigma

It is important not to lose sight of the very real effects of this '*suffusive territorial stigma*'. By the 1950s and 1960s, the tenants of these stigmatised schemes suffered from a battery of cumulative effects. These included being denied credit by High Street stores, difficulties in obtaining a taxi, the refusal of bus-drivers to enter the schemes, being targeted by members of rival gangs, long delays in getting repairs done by the Corporation, hostile policing, and vandalised public telephone kiosks. Further, there could be tragic personal and familial consequences. In *Finding Peggy*, Meg Henderson chronicles the truly horrifying circumstances in 1959 Blackhill whereby her much-loved Aunt Peggy, nine months pregnant and in difficulties in labour, was butchered by an unqualified medical student when her GP refused to attend the delivery, and died as a result.[23] This could never have happened in Mosspark.

Council Housing and Gender

Another issue to which the data on particularly Hamiltonhill and Blackhill point quite clearly is the gendered nature of the council housing market – which the tragedy of Peggy's death exemplifies. It has to be said that by the 1930s, the City Improvements Department was alert to the problem of single-parent families headed by women, and was regularly allocating houses in 'Rehousing' schemes to such families, thus saving them from destitution. As the GPOFA was extremely reluctant to allocate a tenancy to a household headed by a single woman, this was a progressive policy innovation. But the ubiquity of the imaginative coping mechanisms constructed by the women in these schemes alerts us to another issue to do with work. While the local men were coping with their long-term unemployment by thieving, gambling, hard drinking and fighting each other, local women were involved in paid employment as well as domestic labour and collective survival stratagems. For example, Blackhill women worked as cleaners in city centre businesses, the Royal Infirmary and the Royal Technical College (subsequently the University of Strathclyde). But no sooner had they finished waged labour and returned home to the scheme than they had to start all over again, in domestic labour and collective women's struggles. Their housing scheme, and similar ones all over Glasgow, was the site of the classic dual oppression of women. Local men could signify their masculinity by drinking, fighting, gambling and thieving, but it was at the expense of their wives and daughters.

At the end of her evocative article on the literal costs to working-class women of moving out of the slums into the 'Slum-Clearance' scheme of Blackhill, Ann McGuckin says:

> The experiences of these women should not be written off within any theory that equates poverty with powerlessness. That they were poor is true, that they were powerless is not. Within the constraints of poverty they organised and controlled their lives. Most of all they resisted.[24]

It seems to me that McGuckin's emphasis is misplaced. These women's very resistance was forced upon them by overwhelming power and authority. What is lacking here is a notion of agency, of action. The poor always had agency, the potential to act, even if they did not have power. There were always pockets within patriarchal families and communities where state power, local or national, did not reach, and within these pockets the women resisted as best they could, thus challenging the Corporation's notions of 'deserving'. Resistance – whether by rent strikes, self-help through thieving, mutual emotional support, or financial support through menages – was still agency. Although the women of Blackhill were unable to effectively counter-attack the strategic double-bind of patriarchy and capitalist labour-market exclusion which overwhelmed them, they did have agency.

Violence against Women

Further, an extensive literature makes the unavoidable point that such communities were full of domestic violence towards women. The historian of such violence on Clydeside, Annmarie Hughes, has said: 'Inter-war Clydeside spawned a climate in which wife-assault was common and extremely visible.'[25] While this was not a central topic in my research, there can be no doubt that it was and is a very real issue. I asked my old friend, John Nolan, formerly a full-time beat Police Constable in Blackhill from 1972 to 1975, if there was a lot of domestic violence in the scheme. He replied:

> The police substation in Blackhill opened around 1973 (give or take) and I, out of personal interest, checked on wife assault arrests the year before it opened and the year after. As I recall (though the passing of more than 40 years makes these numbers iffy), arrests before were 5 and the year after were 37.
>
> That may sound odd with a permanent police presence in the scheme, but remember that very few people had telephones in those days in Blackhill and so with the new station, neighbours, wives or kids could run into the station and report an assault.
>
> So the answer is yes, wife assaults were common and vastly under-reported ere the station opened. Arrests are also not an accurate guide to numbers, because there was often a change in heart on the part of the victim, resulting in charges not being pressed.[26]

Such considerations contradict the assertion about the power of Blackhill women.

The Victorian Legacy

Victorian bourgeois ideology about the working class, how it was composed, and its housing – or lack of it – was imported uncritically into twentieth-century council housing management in Glasgow, and persisted until the collapse of such housing in the Thatcher years. I will repeat that, as late as 1970, the then Head of Lettings of Glasgow's Housing Management Department (the successor to the City Improvements Department) explained patiently to me, an apparently naïve young sociology graduate, that there were two sections in the working class: the reputable poor and the disreputable poor – and recommended that I read Octavia Hill! The Clerks who dealt with the letting of council houses in the City Improvements Department offices in the Trongate were the direct ideological descendants of the Factors' Clerks of the Victorian years, and displayed the same supercilious attitudes towards council tenants. The Resident Factors in both 'Intermediate' and 'Rehousing' schemes were the direct ideological descendants of the Victorian Factors – and that very word was used until after the Second World War:

> The Manager of the City Improvements Department is responsible for *factoring* all City Improvements property, as well as the municipal houses built by the Housing Department. (My emphasis.)[27]

The City Improvements Department was actually renamed the City Factor's Department in 1950, a singularly unfortunate choice of name.

The subsequent postwar Area Supervisors of Glasgow District Council's Housing Management Department (founded in 1967) were the direct descendants of the Resident Factors. The difference was that these Supervisors did not live in the scheme, but patrolled their area on foot. And the Housing Management Department's (female) Housing Visitors were the direct descendants of the City Improvements Department's Lady Inspectors.[28] What linked them all was an offensive, authoritarian and patriarchal attitude towards the working-class tenants they were supposed to serve. Mary Barbour and John Wheatley might have seen council housing as a social service; Glasgow's housing officials saw council houses as a reluctant bonus which the tenants were lucky to earn.

Glasgow's three-tier league table of housing reflected unapologetic moral judgements, and this was recognised by tenants and housing officials alike. As Brennan said:

> . . . the titles (i.e. Ordinary, Intermediate, Rehousing) also represent an attempt to find inoffensive terms for different gradings of tenant and there is no doubt that until recently they meant 'First Class', 'Second Class', and 'Third Class' tenants respectively.[29]

And, as I suggested earlier, the 'Rehousing' category was pre-stigmatised because it was for slum-dwellers. Brennan again:

> Thus rehousing schemes can be and are recognised as different from the ordinary run of Corporation housing, and tenants who are embarrassed by the stigma attached to the scheme try to move away.[30]

These tenants could 'move away' either by applying for a transfer, doing a 'moonlight flit' back to the private sector, or going to another Local Authority. Now these alleged fractions within the working-class generated by Victorian state economic policy were always signified as homogenous, which they were not. Many skilled manual workers were forced to live in the slums because of the absence of alternative housing. And cyclical employment in the shipbuilding and heavy engineering industries in the decades before the First World War meant that the 'respectable poor' were always only 'a wage away from the gutter', in the Clydeside phrase.

Filtering Up

It is also important to remember that the three tiers of scheme were, theoretically at least, not hermetically sealed. It was Corporation policy from the 1930s onwards to encourage social mobility – 'filtering up', and sometimes 'down' – from 'Rehousing' to 'Intermediate' schemes, and from 'Intermediate' to 'Ordinary', and the reverse. This social mobility was permitted on the basis of having met somewhat opaque criteria of income and fiscal reliability, domestic science expertise, family responsibilities including child-rearing, moral probity and, of course, sobriety. The upward mobility of Mrs H. from the 'Wine Alley' 'Rehousing' scheme to the West Drumoyne 'Intermediate' scheme (discussed in Chapter 4) is a case in point. However, there is no way of knowing the scale of such mobility for the Departmental house-record card system was so disorganised as to be effectively useless (see Appendix II). While the odd figure for a given district is presented in the Annual Reports of the Medical Officer of Health, there is no way of knowing how typical these are. Given the power of housing management ideology, on the one hand, and the sheer demand for council houses, on the other, it seems reasonable to say that this mobility did not involve significant numbers of council tenants in the interwar years. The very nature of mass unemployment and consequent poverty during the Depression would have seen to that. This is not to say that the life-chances of those who were mobile, upwards or downwards, were not significantly affected. It is also apparent that this system of mobility loosened up considerably after the war. However, I retain the strong impression that this whole notion of 'filtering up' was in actual fact an ideological formulation intended to camouflage the fact that it was an uncommon phenomenon. In the course of my research I did not encounter a single tenant who had been downwardly mobile.

The point is that class-based ideology has real power, real persistence and real consequences. But the unintended consequences of this ideology and its imbrication in housing management policy in Glasgow resulted in a post-1919 city clearly segregated by class, and that segregation was much more marked than it was in the Victorian years, when at least there were no 'deserts wi' windaes'. This is not to imply a conspiracy theory within the Corporation. But if you have a category of tenants who are regarded as 'Third Class', that is, effectively undesirable, then logic dictates that only 'Third Class' council housing will be supplied for them. And if housing officials share an ideology which perceives some tenants as 'Third Class', then inevitably and routinely these tenants will be housed in 'Third Class' schemes. It is, therefore, not difficult to see how the Blackhills and 'Wine Alleys' of Glasgow came to have such notoriety for containing only 'riff-raff'. And any questioning of council officials from this period will soon turn up accounts of unofficial and informal attempts to create 'good schemes', or 'good' neighbourhoods within, say, the four huge peripheral schemes. If this is true, then the corollary must also be true, that unofficial sporadic and informal attempts were made to create 'bad' schemes, that is, to use them as 'dumping-grounds' for tenants perceived as 'difficult' in one way or another. As late as 1957, about half the tenants in 'Rehousing' schemes were under some form of official supervision.[31] As Irene Maver said in her history of Glasgow: '. . . the bleak, barrack-like quality of Blackhill contrasted starkly with the cottages of Riddrie, visibly demonstrated the contradictions of inter-war housing strategy'.[32]

This spatial and visual segregation was reinforced by the fact that throughout our period – 1919–56 – political expediency had led to a 'telephone-numbers' mentality, particularly within the Labour Party, which controlled Glasgow. That is, development came to be defined as getting as many council houses up as fast as possible. Brennan recounts the following story:

> Towards the end of the [Second World] war a city councillor attending a joint meeting of local authorities in the Clyde Valley to discuss Glasgow's housing problem, was reported as saying, 'To hell with planning! We want houses!'[33]

While this story may be apocryphal, it has wide currency in local housing circles. And this was as true of the schemes themselves as it was for the city as a whole. As has been demonstrated, once the houses were finished and the roads laid, the schemes were abandoned by the Corporation; the tenants had to lay out and dig the gardens themselves – even in Mosspark.

Postwar Outcomes

This situation was bound to have outcomes in the postwar years. The key immediate postwar legislation was the 1946 Housing Act, which provided 'Ordinary'-type subsidies, that is, subsidies for building houses for the 'general needs' of the working class. This had important implications for the three-tier interwar system, namely that it would have to be substantially modified – although it transpired that there was more continuity than might have been expected. These implications were put into concrete practice by other, associated, considerations. The first was the national recognition that the demobbed servicemen and women who had been fighting Fascism were qualitatively different from the 'heroes' of the First World War. Even although it did continue, blatant class discrimination was more difficult; the population which had voted in the Labour government and the Welfare State had real expectations about their postwar quality of life – including housing. Secondly, this was reinforced by a postwar period of economic expansion along with its attendant revolution of rising expectations. Thirdly, within Glasgow there was an increasing awareness that the interwar three-tier system contained unintended consequences, to wit, ghettoisation. Nevertheless, as has been demonstrated, it did continue in postwar housing schemes like 'The Bundy'.

Thus Glasgow built council housing schemes under 'Ordinary'-type subsidies and categorised them as 'New Ordinary' in the first couple of postwar decades. But in fact what they functioned as were classic interwar 'Intermediate' schemes, housing the mass of manual workers. It is to be remembered that through a process of deliberate and thorough selection, the key white-collar workers and skilled manual workers in the new technologies had been creamed off to populate the New Towns of Cumbernauld and East Kilbride.

Another postwar change was a dramatic easing of the general supervision of council tenants. Again, the strict controls of the interwar period would have been totally unacceptable to a generation of young men and women who had learned a great deal about cleanliness, hygiene, cooking and self- and collective discipline in the Forces. The concrete outcome in postwar Glasgow was the disappearance of the Resident Factors. By the end of the 1960s, they no longer existed. Their function was taken over by the Supervisors, whose role was beefed up to patrol an area of council housing on foot. These changes were signified by the classification of the postwar schemes as 'New Ordinary' – a category which never had Resident Factors. It was as if a whole generation of Glaswegian council tenants had been promoted – as if 'they never had it so good', as the contemporary cliché had it.

An important implication of the decision not to station Resident Factors in the peripheral estates was that thousands of tenants had to make the monthly trip into the City Improvements Department offices in the Trongate to pay their rent. The queues down Argyle Street are remembered to this day. The upshot was that the Department eventually had to employ Collectors to go round the schemes to collect rent. Their vulnerability, and strategic decisions to decentralise certain management functions, led eventually to the establishment of District Offices, which then housed the few remaining local Resident Factors. Senior Factors became Supervisors, the remainder mere Tellers.

The role of Nurse Inspectress was collapsed into that of Housing Visitor in the postwar years, again with an important change of emphasis. Their supervisory role gave way to an inspection role before rehousing. While this role was important in the eventual destination of a new council tenant in the postwar years, and reflected a continuing obsession with social hygiene, the termination of the supervisory role of these women – along with the demise of the Resident Factor – meant that Glasgow's 'Rehousing' schemes were unsupervised.[34] It is hardly surprising that housing 'common sense' in the city places the beginning of the decline and fall of the city's housing schemes, and the rise of 'problem estates', in this period.

Glasgow's immediate post-Second World War housing schemes looked distinctly different from their interwar counterparts. They were largely in tenemental design, but differed from interwar tenements in that they often had balconies, were in very long streets, and many had flat roofs (for example, Craigbank, Priesthill, South Pollok). There was extensive use of systems-building, concrete, and the Corporation's own 'foamslag' blocks. The whole, large-scale construction programme was surrounded by intensive Corporation propaganda, including several films shown nationally on Gaumont-Pathé News.[35] This propaganda did not highlight the gross constructional deficiencies of these schemes, including the fact that the much-vaunted foamslag blocks were highly permeable to water, and the inadequate sound insulation we have documented in Craigbank.

These postwar schemes were huge. Pollok came to contain 9,159 council houses and some 50,000 people – bigger in population terms, as it is often remarked, than some small Scottish towns like Perth or Inverness. The idea of the small, community-sized interwar scheme was abandoned in the rush to get houses up. This is not to say that the peripheral housing schemes did not have distinctive sub-areas, but it is to say that the idea of the housing-scheme-as-integral-community was forgotten. Notions of 'neighbourhood units' were mentioned in connection with the peripheral schemes, but only rhetorically.[36]

Furthermore, the peripheral schemes were constructed without infrastructure, in what can only be described as a comprehensive failure of economic and town planning. The Housing Department got the houses up, and the tenants in, but the tenants arrived to find no shops, no pubs (forbidden in council schemes by a pre-war Corporation by-law), no schools, no doctors, no buses, and frequently no roads.[37] And although the Pollok schemes were theoretically built to house workers in the Hillington industrial estates, there was no parallel systematic selection or allocation policy. In actual fact, once the houses were up in these peripheral schemes, they were all abandoned, and this process has been documented in detail for both Pollok[38] and Castlemilk.[39]

Consequently, the original tenants of the peripheral schemes had a mass of problems to overcome – the schooling of their children, shopping, leisure and travel to work. The Corporation did not exactly abandon them, but it was so preoccupied with its own propaganda about the numbers-game that it frequently forgot its tenants. They responded by creating active if not militant Tenants' Associations, which were then promptly accused of being hotbeds of 'Communism' by the Corporation. The fact of the matter was that they did contain many Communist and Labour Party activists, both men and women – and even the occasional Tory, as we have seen for Craigbank – who were incensed by the Corporation's minimalist interpretation of its job as far as council housing management was concerned. This caveat having been made, Glasgow's postwar tenants shared two important experiences with their interwar predecessors: the first was massive initial satisfaction with their new homes, the second an enthusiastic determination to turn their barren environments into thriving communities, as can be seen in both Craigbank and South Pollok.

One very important component of the council housing system remained unchanged in the first two postwar decades. This was the professional ideology of the local housing managers. This has been characterised as paternalistic to the point of naked authoritarianism. Tenants were seen as items to be allocated to schemes and supervised once there on the basis of 'Father knows best'. But the sheer scale of the postwar housing problem put strains on the bureaucracy of what had become the Housing Management Department. This was resolved by (i) taking on some more staff, and (ii) extending overtime. But neither (the lack of) training nor organisational goals were altered. The thinking in the outside 'age of affluence' may have changed, but there is little evidence of its change in the Corporation of Glasgow. It is small wonder that by the 1960s the contradictions in Glasgow's housing ideology and policy were beginning to crack the bureaucracy wide open. By 1956 a summary of its housing management policy was that it tried, with an evidently declining lack of commitment, enthusiasm and skill, to fit very large numbers of tenants into a rapidly increasing housing stock, with the aid of an ideology whose origins belonged squarely in the mid-Victorian period. Glasgow Corporation then attempted to build its way out of trouble by constructing dozens of high-rise blocks. But that is another 'storey'. Fortunately, Glendinning and Mathesius have made an attempt to account for this high-rise development,[40] while McCall and Mooney have provided a critical analysis of both the construction and demolition of these multis in Glasgow.[41]

House Allocation and Sectarianism

There is one area in which the housing policy of Glasgow Corporation in the inter- and postwar years was a success, and that was, with the exception of the 'Ordinary' schemes, in the avoidance of sectarianism in house allocation. Although unable to pin down any formal decision in the documents (perhaps not surprisingly), it is plain that in the 'Intermediate', 'Rehousing' and postwar 'New Ordinary' schemes, the City Improvements Department was making every effort to achieve balance between Catholics and Protestants.

My interviews consistently threw up the word 'mixed' in the schemes studied. This finding confirms that of Paterson in his study of sectarianism and council house allocation in Glasgow.[42] This was no mean achievement in a city where pessimists feared that sectarian violence might flare as a result of the recent war in Northern Ireland. Where there *was* sectarianism at work in council house allocation was in 'Ordinary' schemes like Mosspark, and the reasons for this have been investigated earlier.

Tenant Satisfaction

It is a measure of the desperate circumstances people had been living in that they were delighted with living in what were in effect so many building sites. It speaks volumes for the resilience of working-class agency that they were able to make such vibrant communities of their new schemes. Glasgow's Medical Officer of Health admitted this as early as 1933 with more than a *soupçon* of astonishment, noting that only *1 per cent* of the people rehoused from the slums 'failed to make good'[43] (my emphasis):

> It could generally be said of the rehoused families that they carried their sense of comradeship with them, retaining their characteristics of mutual help in adversity . . . The majority possessed the desire and the capacity to make the most of this opportunity . . .

Of course they did. Contrary to the offensive epithets of the Professor of Political Economy quoted earlier, human beings are not rats; human beings have agency. And as I have emphasised earlier, all the slum-dwellers wanted from their slums was – out. In distinguishing itself from other forms of history, academic housing history frequently ignores this positive agency. But this is illegitimate. The history of Glasgow council housing is also the history of the agency of council tenants; the language of place is the language of class, and class-struggle. The housing officials of Glasgow, and many of the elected representatives concerned with council housing, stand indicted with, at best, a lack of imagination, and at worst, a cavalier and offensive attitude towards their working-class tenants. These tenants succeeded in making their schemes good places in which to live in spite of their housing managers, not because of them.

Furthermore, to argue that working-class Glaswegians' deprivation, poverty and ill-health are the result of 'unhappiness' is insulting.[44] The implication of this argument is that if working-class locals were only more motivated to take advantage of the individualised opportunities offered by the capitalist system, they would be happier. But people require social and cultural capital to take advantage of the opportunities offered by further and higher education. The young people who live in deprived and stigmatised housing schemes have already been written off; they are not 'deserving' of a place at university. If they are unhappy, they have every right to be, and to blame them for their poverty is merely to add insult to injury. Further, this persistent endeavour to pathologise working-class schemes is to ignore the anxieties, depression, substance abuse and domestic violence in middle-class neighbourhoods and suburbia.

The Politics of Housing on Clydeside

The third part of the answer to the question of the dire nature of Glasgow's housing lies in the red-hot nature of the local politics of housing. Throughout the interwar years, the class-struggle over Glasgow council housing was intense; there was conflict about what kind of housing should be built, where, with what amenities, what the rent should be, who should be allocated houses in the new schemes and how they should be managed. The working-class case was articulated with great skill by the Clydeside ILP. Its continuous and effective agitation on the housing and rents issues resulted in the sensational return of ten of its members as MPs to the House of Commons in 1922, where the campaign continued. The importance of this campaign was because:

> The housing issue always had the potential for mass mobilisation of both men and women of all backgrounds . . . And the ILP as a political party was organically involved with its supporters at a neighbourhood level . . .[45]

On the Clyde, although the ILP and the Labour Party had 50 Councillors out of 113 on the Corporation by the end of 1926,[46] the Moderate Party managed to block successfully all attempts to provide cottage-style housing in the city's 'Intermediate' schemes. Manual workers, however skilled, were deemed unworthy of anything except tenemental council housing. The Moderate Party's followers in the GPOFA also had plenty to say about such housing, and its Minutes for the interwar years are full of hypocritical fulminations against such municipal interference in the free market. For example, in his address to the AGM of 1928, the Chairman said:

> I am sure I voice a general opinion, ladies and gentlemen, when I state that the provision of houses by the municipality should be confined to the poorer paid workers and to tenants dispossessed by slum clearance schemes. This unfortunately does not appear to be the policy of the Corporation, and many subsidised houses are today occupied by people who can afford to pay an economic rent. It is notorious that the tenants comprise Members of Parliament, Town Councillors, public officials and many others in a good position in life, and that in many cases means beyond the amount contemplated when these houses were erected, are evidenced by the possession of motor-cars. It is not right that such people should be subsidised by the general body of rate-payers, and in all such cases the rent charged should bear some proportion to the accommodation given.[47]

And two years later, he is saying:

> There are at the moment hundreds of empty houses in the city, and little or no difficulty is experienced by tenants in finding suitable houses, and in these circumstances it seems to me that the Corporation should discontinue the erection of 3, 4 and 5 apartment houses and confine their attention to the clearance of slum dwellings. The ratepayers of this City are presently paying far too much in local rates, and the day is past when their burden should be increased from year to year to subsidise the tenants of Corporation houses let at uneconomic rents.[48]

Now it has to be admitted that the Chairman has a couple of points. As we have already seen, the first tenants of Mosspark were exactly the kind of people he describes, and this issue was ventilated both at a local level and in Parliament. Further, there were empty houses in Glasgow at this period. But his hypocrisy is evident at three levels. First, in their submissions to both the 1892 Presbytery Commission on the Housing of the Poor and the 1904 Glasgow Municipal Commission on the Housing of the Poor, inter alia, the city's property-owners had been flatly opposed to the rehousing of slum-dwellers. Second, with regard to empty privately owned houses in the city – a point they returned to again and again in the interwar years – they failed to acknowledge that these houses were empty because working-class tenants could not afford to pay the rents at a time of Depression and mass unemployment. And third, what they were really saying was they were opposed to *any* interference with the supposed laws of the free market in housing, and hence their profits. Thus there was a neat contradiction between the members of the GPOFA and their representatives on the Corporation, for the latter had to be seen to support council housing in order to win votes. And this stance also demonstrated a complete disregard for the public health consequences of mass overcrowding in the small if otherwise adequate tenemental houses which they owned and managed. Glasgow's white-collar, black-coated and skilled manual workers didn't care what the GPOFA wanted, they aspired to a new council house in Mosspark or Riddrie or Knightswood.

Both the GPOFA and the Moderate Party also proved obdurate about the employment of the Corporation's Direct Labour Organisation. Founded in 1920 in the light of postwar shortages of construction industry tradesmen, in 1921 it had built the 348 houses in the Drumoyne 'Ordinary' scheme under the 1919 Housing & Town Planning Act both cheaper and of a better quality than private enterprise; in fact the saving was £140 per house.[49] But after building more houses at Polmadie and Langlands, in spite of consistent strong backing by Councillor Paddy Dollan of the ILP it built no more houses until 1933. Every attempt to deploy it was blocked by the Moderates.

The irony is that when Labour took over power in the Corporation in 1933 with the assistance of Paddy Dollan's well-oiled political machine, it more or less replicated the policies of the Moderates as far as housing allocation and management was concerned. It is true that it accelerated the construction of 'Rehousing' schemes, but it continued to reproduce the earlier authoritarian housing management practice. It was as if the ideology about moral worth went so deep that it was impossible to change, so tenants were still allocated the housing they 'deserved'. That is why the perceived social divisions were replicated under Labour control in the different kinds of housing scheme in the post-Second World War years. And that is also why there is the real if unintended consequence of Glasgow always having a disproportionate share of deprived areas concentrated in the 'Rehousing' schemes. Even in 2012, the Scottish Index of Multiple Deprivation (SIMD) showed that the top five most deprived 'datazones' contained schemes like

Possilpark, Keppochhill, Parkhead West and Barrowfield.[50] This stark fact would seem to justify Willie McIlvanney's comment which is the motto for this book: the 'Rehousing' schemes were nothing but punishment parks for the poor, while their tenants were nice people.[51] But this rebounded on Glasgow District Council, for potential tenants were well aware which schemes were stigmatised, and refused to accept a house there.

There was a final unintended consequence of the get-the-council-houses-up-as-fast-as-possible policy. This became an obsession in Glasgow after 1956, when the solution to the housing problem was perceived to be the construction of multi-storey tower blocks. While a discussion of this particular policy is outwith the scope of this book, it became a far-from-magnificent obsession which took over Corporation thinking almost entirely, and resulted in the failures of the Gorbals high flats and Red Road, all of which eventually had to be blown up. The man most associated with this policy was former ILP activist David Gibson, a talented and single-minded Labour Councillor who became Housing Convenor. He was responsible in large measure for the dozens of tower blocks which came to punctuate Glasgow's skyline after the 1950s, bulldozing his way ahead over the objections of the city's Town Planners. One of the latter was to complain:

> Gibson was the man we regarded as the frightening one – a white-faced, intense, driving idealist, absolutely fanatical and sincere, of a kind you couldn't help admiring in a way. He was white with passion about the housing problem – one knew he was a man in a hurry! He saw only the one thing, as far as we could see: how to get as many houses up as possible, how to get as many of his beloved fellow working-class citizens decently housed as possible. We all agreed, but the question was, where, how, and at what speed?[52]

Endgame

What, then, are we to make of this story of Glasgow council housing at a strategic political level? What was the meaning of the stigma attached so routinely and pervasively to certain kinds of housing scheme? While I have suggested three areas in the previous section in an attempt to answer these questions, they are presented for the sake of clarity alone. In actual fact, they are not separate issues; they all articulate. Any sociology of housing in Glasgow has to acknowledge that there is a dialectical relationship between the particular demography of the city; the local ideology about housing legislation, provision, allocation and management; and the local political culture. It is this particular articulation which makes Glasgow's council housing trajectory so unique.

As far as the stigma is concerned, while each individual scheme has its own particular story to tell in terms of local ecological factors, Wacquant argues that the overall function of such stigmatisation is to 'symbolically splinter' working-class consciousness.[53] This seems to me to encapsulate the Glasgow experience very neatly. If the tenants of Blackhill and adjacent Riddrie faced each other off, they were hardly going to co-operate in a joint plan to do something about the aerial pollution of the district by the Provan Gasworks, or the dangers to children posed by the semi-derelict Monkland Canal. If the tenants of the cottages in the 'Ordinary' Drumoyne scheme looked down their noses at those in the tenements of nearby 'Intermediate' West Drumoyne, they were hardly going to co-operate in lobbying for an improved public transport system to the shipyards and engineering works of Govan. If the amateur dramatists of Craigbank thought that the tenants of 'The Bundy' lived in 'South Korea', they were hardly going to ask them to join them in a campaign to do something about the leaking flat roofs, or to tackle the numerous environmental disadvantages of living in Pollok. And the douce tenants of Mosspark were hardly going to ask anyone to join them in anything because they believed they were Glasgow's chosen people. All these tenants are disempowered because they lacked a common language with which they could discuss their common problems, and if they lacked this language then the chances of collective action were minimal. As Hancock and Mooney have put it:

> Like earlier 'moral panics' these notions [stigma, etc.] work to divert attention away from the structural and institutional failures that produce and reproduce poverty, as well as neglecting any sense that the workings of the capitalist economy, whether in a period of crisis or not, also create the conditions for emerging social problems as well as social and economic inequality.[54]

Fascinating as the stories of the individual housing schemes and the agency of their tenants are, it must always be remembered that they are but refractions of wider structural issues of social class. Class is the ubiquitous if silent presence in the history of Glasgow's council housing, and while the 'splintering' may have been symbolic, it had real, concrete effects. The city's economic fortunes changed significantly throughout our period, from Depression to rapid wartime industrial growth, to postwar growth in the new technologies and the diverting of skilled workers to the New Towns, to eventual de-industrialisation. The history of Glasgow's council housing can only be understood in relation to these wider economic and social changes. Housing may not develop in precise phase with the cycles of economic growth and decline, but it is irrevocably part of the dynamics of class in capitalist society. Hanley puts it succinctly: '. . . class is built into our landscape in the form of housing'.[55]

A comprehensive sociology demonstrates that not only did Glasgow Corporation perceive the problem of the slums in the Victorian years as one of social pathology within the working class which required major surgery, but also its accounts of the make-up of slum-dwellers were spurious. The slums of Glasgow, from the Victorian years until after the Second World War, did not contain a homogenous mass of unskilled social degenerates, but a wide occupational population ranging from the most skilled manual workers, through the semi-skilled, right down to the completely unskilled.

Nor was this population unorganised and trapped in a form of Hobbesian cultural chaos. As the literature shows, and as was the case in Glasgow, dense social networks typified these slums. That these networks constituted a culture of survival cannot be denied, but that was forced upon the people by extreme poverty caused by the casualised employment concomitant with the cyclical nature of shipbuilding and heavy engineering production. However, this economic truth – that such production was dependent upon casualised employment – was camouflaged by a pernicious class-based ideology which purported to 'explain away' its effects by blaming the poor for their poverty, and the slum-dwellers for creating the slums. This ideology had deep roots among the Victorian bourgeoisie in Glasgow – and elsewhere in Britain – to the extent that 'everybody knew' that the poor were responsible for their own poverty because of their moral degeneracy, drunkenness and fecklessness.

Their degenerate way of living was alleged to have created the deadly miasma which infected those who entered, to the extent that they abandoned all hope. A consequence was that the 'experts' who dealt with the slum-dwellers – particularly public health officials – rapidly developed an authoritarian social practice based on a false ideology, namely that there were large numbers of people who did not deserve decent housing. This practice has been shown to have been particularly and unapologetically punitive in Glasgow, and informed by the precepts of Calvinism. But ideology not only informs social practice, it limits it as well. So even if some of the individual 'experts' realised that the poor were not responsible for their poverty – and the Socialists of the ILP knew this all along – their ability to develop a more humane social practice was minimal given the hegemony of the bourgeois ideology. In the meantime, the poor developed a culture of survival which was remarkable for its courage, humanity, imagination, resilience and stoicism. This was what sociologists have called 'traditional working-class culture'.

But when what came to be known as council housing was introduced in Glasgow just after the First World War, these authoritarian attitudes and practice were transferred uncritically into the operations of the City Improvements Department, which was responsible for the allocation and management of council housing. Interwar council housing in Glasgow rapidly became grouped into the three-tier league table of 'Ordinary', 'Intermediate' and 'Rehousing' schemes, which meant, effectively, First, Second and Third Class, based on notions of moral worth. The very layout, design and interior equipment of these houses, and their tenanting and management, reflected the class-based judgmental attitudes of the Corporation of Glasgow. The visual aspects of the three different kinds of scheme signified the moral status of their tenants immediately and unmistakably. And, as we have seen, the tenants of the 'Rehousing' schemes were patrolled ruthlessly by the moral police of capitalism. The only thing these schemes lacked was barbed wire; it is not stretching the argument too far to suggest that they were open prisons for their tenants. They were certainly treated like convicts on cultural parole. It is to be stressed that Glasgow was the only city in Britain which created such a uniquely rigid league table of housing schemes. As Lynsey Hanley has said:

> . . . it was the policy of housing different social classes separately, in identifiably separate housing, which gave council estates the poor reputation that has persisted throughout their existence.[56]

And yet, the tenants of both 'Intermediate' and 'Rehousing' schemes brought their cultural resilience with them from the slums, organised themselves socially in their schemes and turned them into cheerful communities in no time at all. We have already seen how Glasgow's Medical Officer of Health noted this, albeit with some astonishment (see p. 154). Nevertheless, the overall unintended consequence of the Corporation's blinkered policy was the reproduction and amplification of social and spatial stratification in the city, with the unwanted but inevitable concentration of apparently permanent clusters of acute poverty and deprivation in 'datazones' concentrated in what had been 'Rehousing' schemes. The obsession with the numbers-game had resulted in great swathes of ugly 'deserts wi' windaes', in which the local Bedouin pursued their allegedly self-destructive lives.

Further, it can be seen from the oral testimony of pioneer tenants presented in this book that they were quite capable of theorising their conditions of existence themselves, if not in the same language as the 'experts'. Their language is more blunt and authentic – and humorous. It is hard to restrain a smile at the characterisation of the 'Green Ladies' as 'Buggy Annie' and 'Panshine'. And many of the tenants had sharp insights into both the positive and negative aspects of the cultures of their schemes. That their voices have not been heard for so long is an indictment of the research of the academics concerned with council housing. Now that such council housing has been residualised, thanks to the policies of the rebarbative Margaret Thatcher, what is now called 'social housing' is in the hands of Glasgow's Housing Associations which, on the face of it, would appear to be more democratically organised. Whether their policies will result in a more equitable spread of tenants in their properties remains to be seen. In the meantime, perhaps we can leave the last word to Robert Burns:

> The best laid schemes o' Mice an' Men
> Gang aft agley,
> An' lea'e us nought but grief an' pain,
> For promis'd joy!

Notes

NB: All references preceded by 'GCA' refer to the Glasgow City Archives.

1. Maver (2000), op. cit., p. 170.
2. Ibid., p. 172.
3. See, for example, Glasser, R. (1986), *Growing Up in the Gorbals*, Chatto & Windus.
4. Rodger, R. (1985), 'Employment, Wages and Poverty in the Scottish Cities 1841–1914', in G. Gordon (ed.), *Perspectives of the Scottish City*, Aberdeen University Press, p. 26.
5. Smart, W. (1902), *The Housing Problem and the Municipality*, University of Glasgow Free Lectures, p. 10, quoted in Damer (1989), op. cit., p. 68.
6. For a full discussion, see Damer (1989), op. cit., pp. 64 and 65.
7. Ibid., pp. 65ff.
8. Best, G. (1973), '"Another Part of the Island": Some Scottish Perspectives', in H. J. Dyos and M. Wolff (eds), *The Victorian City: Images and Realities*, Vol. II, Routledge & Kegan Paul, p. 399.
9. Butt (1971), op. cit.; Damer (1989), op. cit.
10. Damer (1989), op. cit., p. 96.
11. See Hill, O. (1883), *Homes of the London Poor*, London: Macmillan; Darley, G. (1990), *Octavia Hill: A Life*, Constable; and Darley, G. (2004), *Octavia Hill: Social Reformer and founder of the National Trust*, Francis Boutle.
12. The 'miasma' was a nineteenth-century medical 'theory' which asserted that disease was caught by inhaling the foetid air of the slums which had been infected irreversibly by the exhalations of sick people, rotting vegetation and flesh, and faeces and urine. It was as if a real but invisible foul cloud hung motionless over the slums and infected everyone who entered them, not only with physical illnesses like cholera but also 'moral degeneracy'. It was linked with the 'theory of urban degeneration' analysed so brilliantly by Stedman Jones (1971, op. cit., Chap. 6). Although the causes of cholera were discovered in 1854, they proved controversial, and 'miasmatic' notions persisted into the twentieth century. Traces of such ideas can still be found in George Orwell's *Down and Out in London and Paris* (1933). Orwell had an acute bourgeois nose for the smell of poverty. For a discussion, see Sutherland, J. (2016), *Orwell's Nose: A Pathological Biography*, Reaktion Books. I am grateful to Professor Tony Fallick for this reference.

13. Stedman Jones (1971), op. cit.; White, J. (2007): *London in the Nineteenth Century: A Human Awful Wonder of God*, Bodley Head.
14. Plunz, R. (2016), *A History of Housing in New York*, Columbia University Press, rev. edn, p. 13.
15. Ibid., p. 62.
16. Wacquant, L. (2008), *Urban Outcasts: A Comparative Sociology of Advanced Marginality*, Polity Press, p. 271; italics in the original.
17. Damer (1989), op. cit.
18. Ward, C. (1976), 'Introduction' to J. F. C. Turner, *Housing by People*, p. 4.
19. Maver (2000), op. cit., p. 233.
20. Damer, S. (2000), '"Engineers of the Human Machine": The Social Practice of Council Housing Management in Glasgow, 1895–1939', *Urban Studies*, Vol. 37, No. 11.
21. A phrase used by Tory Prime Minister Harold Macmillan in a 1957 speech to the Conservative Party in Bedford. His actual words were, 'Let us be frank about it – most of our people have never had it so good.'
22. For Campbell Bunk, see White, J. (1986), *Campbell Bunk, Islington: The Worst Street in South London Between the Wars*, Routledge & Kegan Paul; for the Seven Dials, see Mayhew, H. (1861), *London Labour and the London Poor*, Griffin, Bohn & Co.; and Dickens, C. (1850), *Sketches by Boz: Illustrative of Every-Day Life and Every-Day People*, Hazell, Watson & Viney.
23. Henderson, M. (1994), *Finding Peggy: A Glasgow Childhood*, Corgi, pp. 268ff.
24. McGuckin, A. (1992), 'Moving Stories: Working-Class Women', in: E. Breitenbach and E. Gordon (eds), *Out of Bounds: Women in Scottish Society 1800–1945*, Edinburgh University Press.
25. Hughes, A. (2002), 'Working-Class Culture, Family Life and Domestic Violence on Clydeside, c. 1918–1939: The View from Below', *Scottish Tradition*, Vol. 27. I am grateful to Anni Donaldson for this reference. For Glasgow, see also Robertson, G. (1970), *Gorbals Doctor*, Jarrolds Publishing. For London, see Ross, E. (1983), 'Survival Networks: Women's Neighbourhood Sharing in London Before World War 1', *History Workshop Journal*, Vol. 15, 1, March.
26. Personal communication, Mr John Nolan, 2017.
27. Glasgow Corporation Housing Department, *Review of Operations, 1919–1947*, 1948, p. 13.
28. Damer, S. and R. Madigan (1974), 'The Housing Investigator', *New Society*, Vol. 29, No. 618, 25 July.
29. Brennan (1959), op. cit., p. 172.

30. Ibid., p. 173.
31. Ibid., p. 172.
32. Maver (2000), op. cit., p. 260.
33. Brennan (1959), op. cit., p. 157.
34. Damer and Madigan (1974), op. cit.
35. These include *Let Glasgow Flourish* (1956); *Progress Report* (1946); and *Our Homes* (1949). See the Scottish Screen Archive for details.
36. The 'Neighbourhood Unit' was a town-planning notion which derived from Unwin's garden suburb ideas. It was essentially a 'self-contained' unit in which arterial roads and shops were at the periphery of the neighbourhood; a school was within children's walking distance; and 10 per cent of the land area was to be used for green, open space. It was never quite clear what the 'self-containment' comprised, and the whole notion has been criticised as constituting some kind of nostalgia for a rural arcadia.
37. See Mooney (1988), op. cit., for a detailed description of this process.
38. Ibid.
39. Castlemilk People's History Group (1990), *The Big Flit: Castlemilk's First Tenants*, Glasgow: Workers' Educational Association.
40. Glendinning, M. and S. Mathesius (1994), *Tower Block: Modern Public Housing in England, Scotland, Wales, and Northern Ireland*, Yale University Press.
41. McCall, V. and G. Mooney (2017), 'The Repoliticisation of High-Rise Housing in the UK and the Classed Politics of Demolition', *Built Environment*, Vol. 43, No. 4.
42. Paterson, I. (2002), 'Sectarianism and Municipal Housing Allocation in Glasgow', *Scottish Affairs*, No. 39, Spring.
43. *Annual Report of the Medical Officer of Health for Glasgow* (Dr McGregor), 1933.
44. Craig, C. (2010), *The Tears That Made the Clyde*, Argyll Publishing. But see my review article of this book: 'The Peculiarities of the Clydesiders', *Scottish Affairs*, No. 74, Winter 2011.
45. Damer (1990), op. cit., p. 125.
46. Maver (2000), op. cit., p. 235.
47. GUA [Glasgow University Archives] UGD 342 1/4: *Minutes* of the Glasgow Property Owners & Factors Association, 26 January 1928, p. 3ff.
48. Ibid., 23 January 1930, p. 6ff.
49. GCA DTC.7.12.2.3: *Review of Operations 1919–1947*, 1948, p. 21.
50. McCrone, D. (2017), *The New Sociology of Modern Scotland*, Sage, p. 183.
51. McIlvanney, W. (1977), *Laidlaw*, Hodder & Stoughton, p. 32.

52. Quoted in Glendinning and Mathesius (1994), op. cit., p. 222.
53. Wacquant (2008), op. cit., pp. 244–7.
54. Hancock, L. and G. Mooney (2013), '"Welfare Ghettos" and the "Broken Society": Territorial Stigmatisation in the Contemporary UK', *Housing, Theory and Society*, Vol. 30, No. 1, p.59.
55. Hanley, L. (2012), *Estates: An Intimate History*, new edn, Granta, p. ix.
56. Ibid., p. 83.

Appendix I

Balloting for a Council House

This Appendix describes the details of the actual process whereby a Glasgow council house was allocated to a specific tenant within our time period. It is an extract from an extended interview with a retired, 91-year-old City Improvements Department official who joined it as a Junior Clerk in 1928, eventually became Head of Lettings, and finally Administrative Officer for the whole Department. His name is a pseudonym.

JL: The Clerk in charge of the letter, the selector, as he or she was known, had his cards marked to indicate whether they [the tenants] were, if they were wanting the West End, or if they had exercised a strong preference for Knightswood or Scotstoun or Kelvindale.

SD: Right. How did it work manually, James, did the selector have a bunch of cards?

JL: Yes, there was a cabinet full of drawers.

SD: Right.

JL: And the cards were in eighteen drawers.

SD: Right. And the top drawer of whatever would have the applicants with the highest number of points? Is that right?

JL: For the size of a house.

SD: Right.

JL: They were graded into three-, four- and five-apartment houses basically.

SD: Right. Let me see if I can reconstruct this. The selector is told – but, first of all – who told your Department that houses were ready?

JL: The Housing Department, as it was then known.

SD: Right, which was still separate from yours?

JL: Yes.

SD: You got a note that there was a –

JL: – number of two-, three-, four- or five-apartment houses in a certain area.

SD: In Barmulloch Drive?

JL: Yes.

SD: Right. So your selector looks at No. 100 Barmulloch Drive, and up the close there are four three-apartment houses.

JL: Yes.

SD: He goes to the drawer for three-apartment houses in his area, and he looks for the first tenants with the highest number of points suited for a three-apartment house. Somebody therefore had to keep these cards up to date.

JL: Yes. The selector.

SD: So the selector was responsible for rank-ordering the cards, and the actual selecting?

JL: Yes.

SD: Some job.

JL: He knew his area, or she knew her area. I've known selectors that went out and paid a visit to an area that was developing so that they would become familiar with it. Though there isn't much point even in inviting someone for interview for a house in Kelvindale if they cannae climb a hill!

SD: Right.

JL: Motorists weren't as common in those days as they are today.

SD: Right, right. James, what would happen if, in No. 100 Barmulloch Drive, there were four three-apartment houses vacant but there were twenty people, applicants, with exactly the same number of points? That must have happened many a time.

JL: Yes. If there were say twelve houses available, or eight houses available, they probably sent for ten or twelve applicants.

SD: Which ten or twelve?

JL: The top ten or twelve.

SD: Supposing there were more than ten or twelve with the same number of points?

JL: Toss up. It rarely happened. It could happen if there were only one or two houses available, but it very, very rarely happened where there were a number of houses available because people expressed a preference even within Springburn – some wanted Balornock and would take Barmulloch as an alternative.

SD: Yes.

JL: But some wouldn't – some didn't want Balornock but wanted –

SD: – Balgrayhill, or wherever.

JL: God aye, nobody wanted Balgrayhill! However, yes, that's true. People exercised their individual preference on their application.

SD: Right. Now, supposing in the 1950s, you got the people, the tenants on the waiting list and the houses pretty evenly matched, how would you decide which tenant got which house?

JL: Balloted.

SD: Balloted. Straightforward ordinary ballot?

JL: Generally speaking. It was rarely there was only one close ready at a time, there could be two or three places.

SD: Right.

JL: And 99 times out of a 100 they all turned up at the ballot.

SD: I'll bet they did.

JL: And they all drew for ground floor, upstairs . . .

SD: What was it, a straw, a piece of paper or what?

JL: Piece of paper.

SD: Right, and the selector did this?

L: The applicant drew the houses.

SD: Yes, but the selector organised the ballot.

JL: Yes, the selector organised it. And the selector didn't, as a rule, go out to the ballot, generally someone more senior than the selector because if there was any dispute on the site, he would probably sort it out on the spot.

SD: Right.

JL: And if someone requiring a ground-floor house, as some of them do –

SD: – for health reasons –

JL: – for health reasons. Then that one would be taken out of the general ballot but allocated a house on the ground floor.

SD: On the ground floor. Right.

JL: And he had to explain to the tenant why that was happening – he or she. Generally speaking it was a man.

SD: Could the tenants, after the ballot, could the tenants swap houses?

JL: Yes.

SD: And that would be perfectly agreeable to the Department?

JL: Yes, so long as it was agreeable to the tenants.

SD: Right.

JL: Because the requirements were the same.

SD: Right. So the missive would not be signed until the tenants had done minor adjustments?

JL: The missives were made out, but not signed by the applicant until the ballot had been completed.

SD: Right. And the subsequent adjustment taken place.

JL: And any subsequent adjustment taken place.

SD: Right.

JL: Not infrequently, someone with young children didnae want to be two stairs up, and the folk who were going to be in below them didnae want them up above them!

SD: Right, so they'd swap.

JL: So they'd swap over, yes.

SD: So would you then change the missive?

JL: The missive didn't need changing.

SD: Oh, I see.

JL: The missive would be made out for the address, the position of the house and the rental.

SD: Right.

JL: Which were fixed.

SD: Right.

JL: And required only the signature of the applicant.

SD: Right. So you would fill in the name of the tenant and get the signature later.

JL: There was no name on the missive, on the original missive.

SD: Oh, I see.

JL: Only a signature.

SD: Right. So it was 0/1, 0/2, 1/1, 1/2 –

JL: – House 2/2, Barmulloch Square, Ground 1, or 1/1.

SD: Right, right.

JL: And the rental as such and such.

SD: Right.

JL: Payable monthly in advance, in theory. And at the foot of the missive there was a space for the signature, the occupation and the present address of the applicant. And they signed that on the spot. Just as if it was a single let, they would do it at the head office.

Appendix 2

Methodological Notes

In the course of this research, several unanticipated methodological problems were encountered. A major problem was that the 'House Record Cards' which were supposed to be maintained for every single council house in Glasgow proved to be a myth. Many of these cards were either dumped or burned in the three major moves of the Housing Management Department since 1919, or were hopelessly misfiled. As a reliable data-source, they were useless. For example, the house-cards for Blackhill were so incomplete as to suggest that the bulk of them had been dumped, officially or unofficially. This was an important setback, for it meant that it was impossible to use them in the reconstruction of tenancy turnover patterns in a given scheme. This also meant that a detailed comparison of the development of Glasgow's council housing with that of Liverpool,[1] which was originally intended, was also impossible. Thus, in reconstructing tenancy turnover patterns, an analysis of the Valuation Rolls was necessary; this was both time-consuming and, of course, unhelpful as far as family characteristics of tenants were concerned.

Another major problem was that the extensive data on original tenants contained in the Draft Rolls was not available for the top grade of housing scheme, the 'Ordinary' schemes. Draft Rolls were kept only for 'Intermediate' and 'Rehousing' schemes, and, even then, only a Sub-Let Book (or 'Rental Roll') was kept for Hamiltonhill. I can only conclude that as this scheme was among the four small experimental 'Slum-Clearance' schemes of Glasgow in the early 1920s, the Draft Roll system had not yet been developed. Further, while there was no Draft Roll for Mosspark, its original occupational structure could be computed from its Sub-Let Book, which exists in the City Archives. The reconstruction of family patterns for this scheme had to be done by interviewing.

A final problem lay in the fact that, in the post-Second World War schemes, tenants' occupations were no longer recorded in the Valuation Rolls. This meant that the changing nature of the social and occupational profiles of postwar schemes could not be charted. The best that could be achieved was a snapshot of the original tenants of these schemes, taken from the data in the Draft Rolls at the time of the original research.

Data on the internal workings of the City Improvements Department were obtained not only from its records, but also through interviews with a number of retired officials. One of them was the key figure interviewed in Appendix 1, while three elderly retired Resident Factors from the interwar period were also interviewed. It is to be noted that numerous serving and retired officials from the Glasgow Corporation City Improvements Department (later City Factor's Department [1950], then Housing Management Department [1967]), were very interested in this research project, and proved more than willing to be interviewed, or to discuss their work. I am most grateful to them.

Note

1. Pooley, G. and S. Irish (1989), *The Development of Corporation Housing in Liverpool 1869–1945*, Resource Paper, Centre for North West Regional Studies, University of Lancaster.

Bibliography

Articles, Books, Theses

Armstrong, G. and M. Wilson (1973), 'City Politics and Deviancy Amplification', in I. Taylor and L. Taylor (eds), *Politics and Deviance*, Penguin Books.

Best, G. (1973), '"Another Part of the Island": Some Scottish Perspectives', in Dyos, H. and M. Wolff (eds), *The Victorian City: Images and Realities*, Vol. II, Routledge & Kegan Paul.

Bolitho, W. (1924), *Cancer of Empire*, Putnam's.

Boyle, J. (1977), *A Sense of Freedom*, Pan.

Bowley, M. (1945), *Housing and the State*, Allen & Unwin.

Branson, N. and M. Heineman (1973), *Britain in the 1930s*, Panther.

Brennan, T. (1959), *Reshaping a City*, House of Grant.

Burnett, J. (1986), *A Social History of Housing*, Methuen.

Butt, J. (1978), 'Working-Class Housing in Glasgow, 1900–1939', in I. McDougall (ed.), *Essays in Scottish Labour History*, John Donald.

Castlemilk People's History Group (1990), *The Big Flit: Castlemilk's First Tenants*, Workers' Educational Association.

Chalmers, A. (1905), *Public Health Administration in Glasgow: A Memorial Volume of the Writings of James Burn Russell, B.A., M.D., Ll.B.*, James MacLehose & Sons.

Checkland, S. (1967), *The Mines of Tharsis: Roman, French and British Enterprise in Spain*, Allen & Unwin.

Checkland, S. (1981), *The Upas Tree*, University of Glasgow Press, 2nd edn.

Corporation of Glasgow (1923), *Glasgow: Its Municipal Undertakings and Enterprises*.

Cramond, R. (1964), *Allocation of Council Houses*, University of Glasgow Social & Economic Studies Occasional Paper No. 1, Oliver & Boyd.

Crawford, R. (2013), *On Glasgow and Edinburgh*, The Belknap Press of Harvard University Press.

Damer, S. (1980), 'State, Class and Housing: Glasgow 1885–1919', in J. Melling (ed.), *Housing, Social Policy and the State*, Croom Helm.

Damer, S. (1989), *From Moorepark to 'Wine Alley': The Rise and Fall of a Glasgow Housing Scheme*, Edinburgh University Press.

Damer, S. (1990), *Glasgow: Going for a Song*, Lawrence & Wishart.

Damer, S. (1992), *'Last Exit to Blackhill': The Stigmatisation of a Glasgow Housing Scheme*, University of Glasgow Centre for Housing Research Discussion Paper No. 37.

Damer, S. (2000), '"Engineers of the Human Machine": The Social Practice of Council House Management in Glasgow, 1895–1939', *Urban Studies*, Vol. 37.

Damer S. and L. Hartshorne (1991), 'Habitat et Réputation: Peur et Sentiment de Dégoût dans les Logements Sociaux de Glasgow', *Déviance et Société*, Vol. 15, No. 3.

Damer, S. and R. Madigan (1974), 'The Housing Investigator', *New Society*, Vol. 29, No. 618, 25 July.

Daunton, M. (1990), *Housing the Workers: A Comparative Perspective*, Leicester University Press.

Dickens, C. (1850), *Sketches by Boz: Illustrative of Everyday Life and Everyday People*, Hazell, Watson & Viney.

Donzelot, J. (1979), *The Policing of Families: Welfare Versus the State*, Hutchinson.

Fyfe, P. (1899), *Housing of the Labouring Classes*, Robert Anderson.

Gaitens, E. (1948), *The Dance of the Apprentices*, Canongate.

Gallagher, T. (1987), *Glasgow: The Uneasy Peace: Religious Tensions in Modern Scotland*, Manchester University Press.

Gibb, A. (1982), *The Development of Public Sector Housing in Glasgow*, University of Glasgow Centre for Urban & Regional Research Discussion Paper No. 6, Glasgow.

Gibb, A. (1983), *Glasgow: The Making of a City*, Croom Helm.

Glasser, R. (1986), *Growing Up in the Gorbals*, Chatto & Windus.

Glendinning, M. and S. Mathesius (1994), *Tower Block: Modern Public Housing in England, Scotland, Wales and Northern Ireland*, Yale University Press.

Goldthorpe, J., D. Lockwood, F. Bechhofer and J. Platt (1969), *The Affluent Worker in the Class Structure*, Cambridge University Press.

Hancock, L. and G. Mooney (2013), '"Welfare Ghettos" and the "Broken Society": Territorial Stigmatisation in the Contemporary UK', in *Housing, Theory and Society*, Vol. 30, No. 1.

Hanley, C. (1984), *Dancing in the Streets*, Corgi.

Hanley, L. (2012), *Estates: An Intimate History*, Granta.

Henderson, M. (1994), *Finding Peggy: A Glasgow Childhood*, Corgi.

Horsey, M. (1990), *Tenements and Towers: Glasgow Working-Class Housing 1890–1990,* HMSO.

Hughes, A. (2002), 'Working-Class Culture, Family Life and Domestic Violence on Clydeside, c. 1918–1939: The View From Below', in *Scottish Tradition*, Vol. 27.

Jones, G. Stedman (1989), *Outcast London: A Study in the Relationships Between Classes in Victorian London*, Penguin Books.

Law, A. and G. Mooney (2011/12), '"Poverty Porn" and *The Scheme*: Questioning Documentary Realism', in *Media Education Journal*, 50, Winter.

McArthur, A. and H. Kingsley Long (1935), *No Mean City*, Longmans, Green.

McCall, V. and G. Mooney (2017), 'The Repoliticisation of High-Rise Housing in the UK and the Classed Politics of Demolition', *Built Environment*, Vol. 43, No. 4.

McCrone, D. (2017), *The New Sociology of Modern Scotland*, Sage.

McDougall, I. (1978) (ed.), *Essays in Scottish Labour History*, John Donald.

MacGregor, Sir A. (1967), *Public Health in Glasgow, 1905–1937*, E. & S. Livingstone.

McGuckin, A. (1992), 'Moving Stories: Working-Class Woman', in E. Breitenbach and E. Gordon (eds), *Out of Bounds: Women in Scottish Society 1800–1945*, Edinburgh University Press.

McIlvanney, W. (1977), *Laidlaw*, Hodder & Stoughton.

McKean, C. (1993), 'Between the Wars', in P. Reed (ed.), *Glasgow: The Forming of a City*, Edinburgh University Press.

Maclennan, D. and A. Gibb (1988), *Glasgow: No Mean City to Miles Better*, University of Glasgow Centre for Housing Research Discussion Paper No. 18, Glasgow.

Malpass, P. (2015), *Housing and the Welfare State: The Development of Housing Policy in Britain*, Routledge & Kegan Paul.

Maver, I. (2000), *Glasgow*, Edinburgh University Press.

Maver, I., 'Neighbourhoods', www.theglasgowstory.com. Accessed 23 November 2017.

Mayhew, H. (1861), *London Labour and the London Poor*, Griffin, Bohn & Co.

Merrett, S. (1979), *State Housing in Britain*, Routledge & Kegan Paul.

Mooney, G. (1988), *Living on the Periphery: Housing, Industrial Change and the State*, unpublished PhD Thesis, University of Glasgow.

Morgan, N. (1989), '"£8 Houses for Glasgow citizens": Innovations in municipal house-building in Glasgow in the inter-war years', in R. Rodger (ed.), *Scottish Housing in the Twentieth Century*, Leicester University Press.

Orwell, G. (1933), *Down and Out in London and Paris*, Penguin Books.

Paterson, B. (2008), *Tales From the Back Green*, Hodder & Stoughton.

Paterson, I. (2002), 'Sectarianism and Municipal Housing Allocation in Glasgow', *Scottish Affairs*, No. 39, Spring.

Patrick, J. (1973), *A Glasgow Gang Observed*, Neil Wilson Publishing.

Plunz, R. (2016), *A History of Housing in New York*, Columbia University Press.

Pooley, G. and S. Irish (1989), *The Development of Corporation Housing in Liverpool, 1869–1945*, Resource Paper, Centre for North-West Regional Studies, University of Lancaster.

Robertson, G. (1970), *Gorbals Doctor*, Jarrolds Publishing.

Rodger, R. (1989), *Scottish Housing in the Twentieth Century*, Leicester University Press.

Ross, E. (1983), 'Survival Networks: Women's Neighbourhood Sharing in London Before World War 1', *History Workshop Journal*, Vol. 15, 1, March.

Sennett, R. and J. Cobb (1993), *The Hidden Injuries of Class*, New York: Knopf.

Smart, W. (1902), *The Housing Problem and the Municipality*, University of Glasgow Free Lectures.

Sutherland, J. (2016), *Orwell's Nose: A Pathological Biography*, Reaktion Books.

Swenarton, M. (1981), *Homes Fit for Heroes: The Politics and Architecture of Early State Housing in Britain*, Heinemann Educational.

Taylor, A. (ed.) (2016), *Glasgow: The Autobiography*, Birlinn.

Treble, J. (1978), 'The Market for Unskilled Labour in Glasgow, 1891–1914', in McDougall (ed.), op. cit.

Unwin, R. (1909), *Town Planning in Practice: An Introduction to the Art of Designing Cities and Suburbs*, Ernest Benn.

Wacquant, L. (2008), *Urban Outcasts: A Comparative Sociology of Advanced Marginality*, Polity Press.

Ward, C. (1976), 'Introduction', in J. Turner, *Housing by People*, Marion Boyars.

Weir, M. (1971), *Shoes Were for Sunday*, Macmillan.

White, J. (1986), *Campbell Bunk, Islington: The Worst Street in South London Between the Wars*, Routledge & Kegan Paul.

White, J. (2007), *London in the Nineteenth Century: A Human Awful Wonder of God*, Bodley Head.

Young, M. and P. Willmot (2007), *Family and Kinship in East London*, Penguin Books.

Documents Held in the Glasgow City Archives & Special Collections, Mitchell Library

Damer, S. (1991), *A Social History of Glasgow Council Housing, 1919–1965*, Report on ESRC Research Project No. R000231241, University of Glasgow Centre for Housing Research, August.
Damer, S. (1991), *Housing Scheme Reports*, Appendix II to Report, loc. cit.
Minutes of the Corporation of Glasgow.
Question Books of the Corporation of Glasgow.
Corporation of Glasgow (1923): *Glasgow: Its Municipal Undertakings and Enterprises.*
Corporation of Glasgow Housing Department (1927): *Review of Operations 1919–1927.*
Corporation of Glasgow Housing Department (1937): *Review of Operations 1919–1937.*
Corporation of Glasgow Housing Department (1948): *Review of Operations 1919–1947.*
Hansard: House of Commons Debates.
Yearbooks of the Glasgow Citizens Union.
D-TC 8/18: 1919–1921, 1921–1922, 1923–1924.
D-CF/3/1.
D-CF 1.3.
D-HE/1/1/21.
D-HE/1/5/35-37.
D-HE/4/1/7.
D-HE/5/3/17.
D-HE/6/7/139.
D-HEW 18/1.
PA3/168.
TD6 17/1 & 2.

Documents Held in Glasgow University Archives

UGD 342 1/4.

Newspapers, Magazines

The Baillie
Daily Record

Evening Times
Forward
Glasgow Eastern Standard
Glasgow Herald
Govan Press

Index

Note: references to images are in *italics*; reference to notes are indicated by n

CPSIA information can be obtained
at www.ICGtesting.com
Printed in the USA
JSHW041157061120
9341JS00001B/13

9 781474 440578